The Sparkling Story of Coca-Cola

Gyvel Young-Witzel & Michael Karl Witzel

An Entertaining History Including Collectibles, Coke Lore, and Calendar Girls

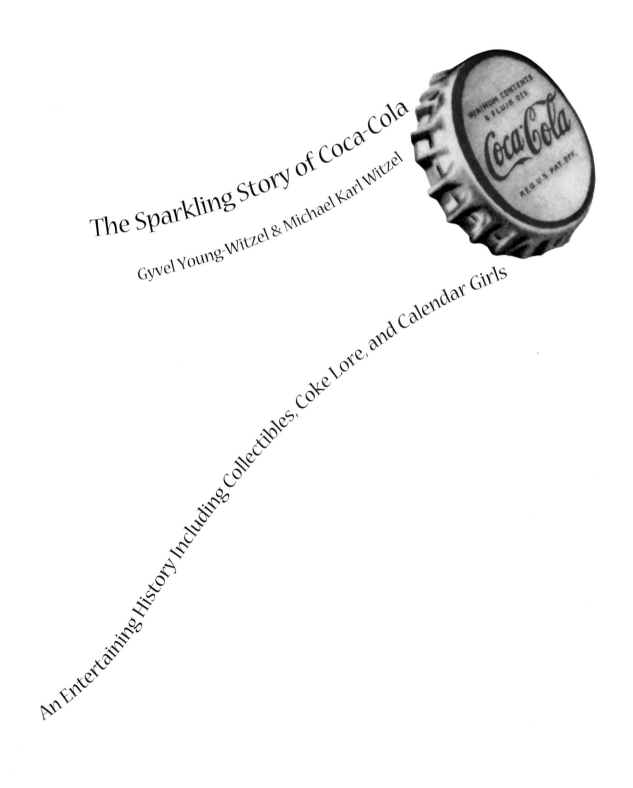

The Sparkling Story of
Coca-Cola

An Entertaining History Including Collectibles, Coke Lore, and Calendar Girls

by Gyvel Young-Witzel
and Michael Karl Witzel

CRESTLINE

Dedication

For our friend Zeppelin, we miss you . . .

Bristol Coca-Cola Wall Sign

Endsheets: This bold example of a Coca-Cola wall sign hails from Bristol, Connecticut, not Bristol, England. The three gents who posed for the photo are no doubt involved with the business end of this establishment. Hammer's Drug Store had a soda fountain . . . and they wanted people to know about it. *Courtesy of The Coca-Cola Company*

1909 Here's a Glass Calendar

Page 2: "Here's a Glass" was the slogan used in 1909, coupled with the ever-popular pretty girl. That year, there were approximately 379 bottlers of Coca-Cola in operation. Coke was growing, and ads like these tempted new customers to take a chair an have a drink! *Courtesy of The Coca-Cola Company*

Flandermeyer's Pharmacy

Page 3: "Summer and Winter, At Our Fountain" was probably not an official advertising slogan originated by the Coca-Cola Company. Nevertheless, it served H. H. Flandermeyer's Pharmacy just fine, providing a succinct slogan to draw customers into the store. The advertising billboard was painted by Pittsburgh's Pennsylvania Advertising Company. *Preziosi, Coolstock.com*

The World Loves Coca-Cola Cutout

Page 6: This "All The World Loves a Coca-Cola" advertising cutout appeared in 1904, years before the 1971 "I'd Like to Buy the World A Coke" ads captured the imagination of the cola drinkers everywhere. *Courtesy of The Coca-Cola Company*

This edition published in 2013 by CRESTLINE
a division of BOOK SALES, INC.
276 Fifth Avenue Suite 206
New York, New York 10001 USA

This edition published by arrangement with Voyageur Press, Inc.
400 First Avenue North, Suite 400, Minneapolis, Minnesota, 55401

Text copyright © 2002 by Gyvel Young-Witzel and Michael Karl Witzel

Edited by Kari Cornell
Designed by JoDee Turner
Printed in China

10   9   8   7   6   5   4   3   2
Reprinted 2013

Library of Congress Cataloging-in-Publication Data

Young-Witzel, Gyvel, 1948–
    The sparkling story of coca-cola : an entertaining history including collectibles, coke lore, and calendar girls / by Gyvel Young-Witzel and Michael Karl Witzel.
        p. cm.
Includes bibiographical references and index.
    ISBN 978-0-7858-2919-5
    1. Coca-Cola Company—Collectibles. 2. Advertising specialties—United States. 3. Advertising—Carbonated beverages. 4. Coca-Cola Company—History.   I. Witzel, Michael Karl, 1960- II. Title.
    NK808.Y686 2002
    338.7'66362—dc21

2002002563

Acknowledgments

Thank you to the following individuals, organizations, photographers, collectors, enthusiasts, and companies that provided many of the invaluable resources required to complete this book: Jennifer Andrews, Public Relations Officer, Cadbury Schweppes Public Limited Company, London, England; Rebecca A. Berkley, Photographic Research, Cadbury Schweppes, Public Limited Company, London, England; Lisa Berger Carter, Associate Coordinator, Rights and Reproductions, The New York Historical Society, New York, New York; Marie Cavanagh, Director, Information Services, National Soft Drink Association, Washington, D.C.; The Coca-Cola Company, Atlanta, Georgia; Coolstock, Inc., www.coolstock.com; Dr Pepper/Cadbury North America, Dallas, Texas; Mark Foster, Pepsi-Cola Meeting Services, Pepsi-Cola Company, Somers, New York; Holly H. Hallanan, The George S. Bolster Collection of the Historical Society of Saratoga Springs, Saratoga Springs, New York; Gordon Harper, The Design Studio, Cadbury Limited, Bournville, Birmingham, England; Wendy Haynes, Coordinator, Rights and Reproductions, The New York Historical Society, New York, New York; Imagers, Digital Production Center, Atlanta, Georgia; Larry Jabbonsky, Public Relations Department, Pepsi-Cola Company, Somers, New York; Joan Johnson, Circa Research & Reference, Seattle, Washington; Brookie Keener, Archives Department, The Coca-Cola Company, Atlanta, Georgia; William P. Kloster, Dr Pepper Bottling Co., Museum & Soda Fountain, Dublin, Texas; The Library of Congress, Washington, D.C.; Dora McCabe, Group Public Relations Manager, Cadbury Schweppes Public Limited Company, London, England; Alexandra McKee, The George S. Bolster Collection of the Historical Society of Saratoga Springs, Saratoga Springs, New York; National Soft Drink Association, Washington, D.C.; National Museum of American History, Center for Advertising History, Smithsonian Institution, Washington, D.C.; John R. Paul, Author, *Soft Drink Bottling,* Springfield, Illinois; Amanda Pittaway, The Design Studio, Cadbury Limited, Bournville, Birmingham, England; Don & Newly Preziosi, Preziosi Postcards, Mendham, New Jersey; Royal Crown Company, Incorporated, Ft. Lauderdale, Florida; Milo Stewart, New York State Historical Association, Cooperstown, New York; Rick Sweeney, Painted Soda Bottles Collectors Association, La Mesa, California; William B. Tilghman, Vice President/Technical Director, Big Red, Incorporated, Waco, Texas; Catherine VanEvans, Cadbury Schweppes Incorporated, Dallas, Texas; Anthony G. van Hayningen, Manager, Environmental Affairs, National Office, Canadian Soft Drink Association, Toronto, Ontario; Jeff Walters, Memory Lane Publishing, Author, *Classic Soda Machines,* Camino, California; Ellen Zimny, Consumer Affairs Specialist, The Coca-Cola Company, Atlanta, Georgia.

Over 60 Million Blotter
The golden age of bottled beverages was a tasty (and profitable) time. Long before wax-coated paper cups with plastic lids were even dreamed of, soft drink companies packaged products-to-go in glass. Since the bottles could be returned to any sales outlet for a cash rebate, people who were down on their luck could scour the street sides for castoffs and earn some quick pocket money. This early form of recycling made sense. With sixty million bottles of Coca-Cola consumed in just one day, collecting empties promised to be a lucrative industry for 1960s scavengers. *Coolstock.com Advertising Archives*

Contents

Introduction

Welcome to America, Land of Coca-Cola

Boys Drinking Pop

Facing page: During the 1950s, drinking a bottle of soda pop after school became a rite of passage for American youth. In the days when all that mattered was school, best friends, and who was going to win the World Series, a cold bottle of pop satisfied the thirst like in no other time in one's life. Coca-Cola capitalized on this fact, making sure their posters and window displays were always within sight. *National Archives via Coolstock.com*

Worldwide Symbol of Friendship

Right: During the 1960s, the McKann Erickson ad agency debuted television commercials that featured a chorus of young people gathered from around the globe, holding hands in a circle. Singing a universal song of Coke à la "I'd Like To Teach The World To Sing," the suggestion was that anyone could access peace, love, harmony, and good times just by buying a cold bottle of Coke. This "Symbol of Friendship" print ad was an early precursor to this idea of global soda serendipity. *Courtesy of The Coca-Cola Company*

Symbol of Friendship

When I was nine years old, my parents moved from Copenhagen, Denmark, to Norfolk, Virginia. I couldn't speak very much English and had yet to start school. With aunts, uncles, grandparents, and cousins left behind, my parents were the only people I knew in this new world. I would have to make new friends—fast.

Although we had no television set, it was clear that Coca-Cola was a big deal over here in America. As we traveled around our new home, Coca-Cola ads and signs were everywhere we looked. Coca-Cola billboards and hand-painted signs appeared along the roadways. Greasy spoon diners and other local mom-and-pop restaurants were festooned with gleaming metal Coke signs, neon signs that flashed the familiar Coca-Cola script logo, and Coca-Cola calendars and serving trays. At neighborhood gas stations and businesses, shiny red Coke machines tempted passersby to try the delicious soft drink. And when we went to the grocery store, green, shapely Coca-Cola bottles seemed to be stacked everywhere.

Just a short bike ride away from where we lived was a corner candy store stocked with Coca-Cola. I often marveled at the number of wooden cases filled with empty bottles that the store owner had placed on the curb to be picked up by a uniformed man in a big truck bearing the Coca-Cola name in red and white. Although I couldn't read the words in English, I had a feeling that the bright red decorative letters of the Coca-Cola logo represented something good.

Having just crossed the Atlantic Ocean from such a small country as Denmark, my senses had yet to adjust to the cavalcade of advertising

images I now saw each day. In those years, advertising was modest in Scandinavia, and I wasn't accustomed to seeing immense billboards and advertising signs posted everywhere the eye could see.

So, what was this drink that garnered so much attention? It must be quite special. My only point of reference for such a treat were the marzipan candies, strong black licorice, and pastries such as *weinerbrød* that I enjoyed in my native land. From the looks of it, Coca-Cola had to be better than all of these goodies combined!

One fateful day my dad picked up a handy six-pack of Coke from the store. Now I would find out what made this drink so special. Back then, a soft drink like Coca-Cola was a special treat to be consumed one small six-and-one-half-ounce bottle at a time. A six-pack might have lasted for an entire month! There were no "super-sized" drinks or "big gulps" that fast-food restaurants and convenience stores offer today. As a kid, you were quite lucky if your parents let you have one bottle of bubbly beverage on occasion. Of course, when you had the extra pocket change you could buy a bottle from a machine, and that really was a big deal.

That same day, I met a girl in the neighborhood and asked if she would like to come over and have a Coke with me. She readily accepted my invitation and we scurried into the kitchen. I pulled a pair of cold bottles from the Frigidaire and hastily popped the tops with a bottle opener. I knew I was going to be in hot water for drinking my dad's Coke, but couldn't seem to stop myself. We guzzled down our delicious Cokes, laughing and having a great time.

I don't remember what was so funny or why we had such a ball. But my newfound Coke-drinking buddy quickly became one of my best friends, as did other kids in the neighborhood. I couldn't speak English very well, but with Coke that didn't seem to matter. Coca-Cola seemed to bridge the communication gap. I figured things out fast in this new land: Whenever I wanted to win over new kids on the block, all I had to do was invite them over for a bottle of Coke. The rest was easy. With a bottle of Coca-Cola in hand, two complete strangers from different cultures had something in common.

Today, I have no trouble communicating, yet I still defer to Coca-Cola as the drink of choice. At family gatherings, at weekend barbecues, and on pizza night, I always serve Coca-Cola.

In the spirit of friendship that goes hand in hand with a bottle of Coca-Cola, I invite you to browse through the chapters of this book, enjoy the colorful advertisements and collectibles, and revel in the wonder of all that American enterprise and ingenuity have to offer. And as you explore the legend that is Coca-Cola, remember that we will be doing it together, as friends, sharing a frosty bottle. Pop . . . fizzzzzz . . . aaaaah! This is *The Sparkling Story of Coca-Cola: An Entertaining History Including Collectibles, Coke Lore, and Calendar Girls.*

October 22, 2001
Gyvel Young-Witzel
Austin, Texas

Coca-Cola Thermometer
The year 1941, when this promotional thermometer debuted, was one of change, not only for the nation but also for the Coca-Cola Company. The year began with an unprecedented advertising budget of more than ten million. By December, the drink's popular nickname "Coke" had become an accepted part of advertising, making its first appearance on bottles. The December 7 attack on Pearl Harbor prompted the Coca-Cola Company's president to announce: "We will see that every man in uniform gets a bottle of Coca-Cola for five cents wherever he is and whatever it costs." *Courtesy of The Coca-Cola Company*

Chapter 1

The Birth of an American Flavor

A One-Gulp History of the Early Days

Coca-Cola Ad, Circa 1905

Facing page: By 1900, pressure from the Anti-Saloon League of America, a temperance organization, forced many saloon keepers to close their doors. Others renovated and reopened as soda fountains. By 1916, twenty-one states had banned saloons, and the soda fountain business boomed. For the first time in history, men, women, and children could enter the same social establishment, walk up to the bar, and order refreshing non-alcoholic beverages together. *Courtesy of The Coca-Cola Company*

High Rock Spring Dipper Boy

Right: Layers and layers of insoluble carbonate deposits formed the unique volcano-like mound of High Rock Spring. Dipping boys plunged glasses at the end of long-handled dippers into the spring to serve the eager crowd. The bubbling waters they dispensed were free but the dipper boys worked for tips. *George S. Bolster Collection of the Historical Society of Saratoga Springs*

T he theme song of the television program *The Beverly Hill-billies* tells the story of a fortuitous event:

"An' then one day, he was shootin' at some food,
an' up through the ground came a bubblin' crude.
Oil that is! Black gold! Texas tea!
Well, the first thing ya know, Jed's a millionaire
Kin-folk said, 'Jed, move away from there.' Said
Californy is the place y'oughta be, so they
loaded up the truck, and they moved to Beverly.
Hills that is! Swimmin' pools, Movie stars!"

The first people to discover the Earth's natural bubbling springs—mineral water that is—probably felt that same sense of surprise and excitement. Here was liquid gold . . . bubbling up from the ground in the form of clear, fresh water!

The biggest surprise of all was that not all springs flowed with plain water. Some were charged with tiny bubbles! The brave souls who drank the waters from these fountains found that each spring had its own distinct flavor, and, best of all, drinking the water did not kill them. In fact, drinking the water seemed to make them feel better.

Before long, rumors of mineral water's amazing healing powers began to circulate. The health of those who regularly consumed the magical waters seemed to improve. A number of people began to drink from the springs with great fervor. Others went so far as to bathe in the waters. Like attendees of a religious tent-revival, the optimistic flocked to the waters in hopes of finding physical redemption.

By the sixteenth and seventeenth centuries, the mystical fervor surrounding these waters gave way to a more scientific approach. Physicians and scientists of the day studied the validity of the water's curative powers and discovered that each source of spring water contained its own unique concentration of minerals. In addition, this mix of mineral salts and trace elements resembled the chemical composition of all living things. Researchers concluded that the human body easily assimilated the mineral water. The water's properties appeared to help the body reconstruct damaged cells.

The scientific world gave the mineral waters a nod of approval and its use as a beverage and as bathing water soared in popularity. Almost immediately, the speculators rushed in. Selling the natural water, a product that seemed to be available in limitless quantities, appeared to be the best moneymaking scheme around. Some embarked on building elaborate spas, others decided to bottle the curative liquid and distribute the product throughout Europe, still others tried their hand at doing both.

Saratoga Arondack Water
The Arondack Spring of Saratoga, New York, drilled in 1872, was originally named the Hypernion Spring. In 1887, the company changed its name to Saratoga Kissingen (after the Bavarian waters). A few years later the French government brought a lawsuit against the Saratoga Vichy Company for using the "Vichy" name without permission. Fearing a similar lawsuit from the Bavarian government the Saratoga Kissingen Company quickly changed its name to Saratoga Arondack Water. (Circa 1900) *Coolstock.com Collection*

Saratoga Springs Pavilion, 1875

The Mohawk Indians originally discovered the naturally carbonated waters of Saratoga Springs, New York. They considered the waters a gift from the god Manitou and kept their location a closely guarded secret. This tranquil state of affairs ended in 1758. After a lengthy land dispute, the Mohawk Indians turned the area that contained the springs over to settlers. Still, the location of the springs remained secret until they were officially discovered in 1770. By the 1850s, the swampy wilderness of Saratoga Springs was transformed into a bustling resort with luxury hotels, genteel amusements, and fancy drinking pavilions. By 1875, crowds of guests gathered at pavilions to drink the healing waters. *George S. Bolster Collection of the Historical Society of Saratoga Springs*

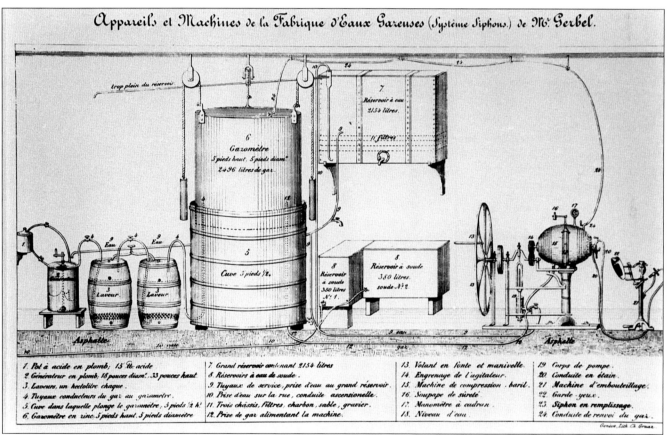

Principles of Jacob Schweppe's

This 1858 illustration describes the principles of the semi-continuous "Geneva System" developed by Jacob Schweppe, circa 1780. This system consisted of a carbon dioxide generator, a gasometer, and a pump that forced the carbon gas into a carbonating chamber, where it mixed with the liquid. When the liquid was thoroughly carbonated, it was drawn off, and the operation was repeated again. *Courtesy of Cadbury Schweppes p.l.c.*

Drills hammered into the earth and tapped into the springs. Workers installed a system of pipes and tubes to carry the healing waters into grand buildings. Notable architects designed many of these structures in the style of the buildings popular in ancient Rome. These replicas of the old Roman baths featured Corinthian columns, marble floors, and ornate faucets. Their sole purpose was to showcase a spa's drinking pavilions and baths.

In these opulent surroundings, guests could sit and relax while they sipped their "medicine." To be "cured," guests sometime endured four-week treatments. For a hefty price, guests had access to private rooms, wholesome meals, massage therapy, mineral baths, nurses, and a staff physician. The staff encouraged guests to stroll along the paths that cut through lush grass and sculpted gardens of the spa's exercise grounds. Strains of live music accompanied guests as they strolled under shade trees and hanging gardens.

While the spas serviced the wealthy and refined gentry, plants that bottled the spring water targeted a broader base of consumers. Entrepreneurs pumped mineral water up through a system of underground pipes directly into bottling machinery where the water was bottled and corked. Spring operators shipped the bottled water to upscale restaurants and pharmacies.

Vichy Water, 1893
One of the world's most famous spa areas is the Vichy hot mineral springs of central France. These thermal waters are promoted as a restorative for those with liver and stomach disorders. For those unable to afford the trip to France there is an alternative: a bottle of Vichy water exported directly from the source. To promote this bottled French export, the Vichy Company of France gave out free samples and souvenir pamphlets at the World's Columbian Exposition of Chicago in 1893. *Coolstock.com Collection*

By this time, scientists were searching for a way to duplicate the chemical make-up of natural mineral waters. Many scientists hoped that this "copy" would provide a cheaper alternative to the expensive natural waters, which would allow consumption and enjoyment of mineral water for the masses.

In 1767, British chemist Joseph Priestly was the first to successfully duplicate the carbonation found in natural spring water. Another Brit, Dr. John Mervin Nooth, astonished the Royal Society of London in 1774 when he unveiled his latest invention—a simple apparatus that added carbonation to water.

Swedish chemist Torben Bergman discovered that each type of salt inherent in mineral water benefited the human body in a different way. With that in mind, physicians began to prescribe waters that contained alkaline salts to treat digestive problems, rheumatism, and gout. Doctors used sulfur waters to treat of infectious diseases, including leprosy and syphilis. The waters containing lithium seemed to help those with mental disorders.

Jacobs' Pharmacy

Before long, soda fountains had sprung up to supply mineral water in a variety of flavors to the thirsty masses. Willis Venable, the self-proclaimed "Soda Water King of the South," operated this twenty-five-foot marble extravaganza on the ground floor of Jacobs' Pharmacy. In May 1886, the first glass of Coca-Cola fizzed to life under the pillared canopy of this fountain counter. The unique blend of spices, citrus, and combined properties of the coca leaf and kola nut gave the drink its distinct flavor. The fountain continued to serve parched Atlanta citizens until early 1960. Later in the decade, the pharmacy was demolished to make way for a bank and an office building. *Courtesy of The Coca-Cola Company*

Bergman's discovery helped scientists who wanted to create their own artificial mineral water. It didn't take long for pharmaceutical entrepreneurs to begin producing the artificial mineral water for public use. Stomach ache? Just take a trip to your local apothecary and buy a bottle of the type of mineral salts believed to settle the digestive system.

Artificially carbonated mineral water was the true hit of the apothecary. The same companies that manufactured bottling equipment also sold carbonation equipment that could be housed in the basements of pharmacies. Although the equipment was large, cumbersome, and ugly, it produced the desired affect: a glass of pure, bubbling water. At the time, pure water was hard to come by. Water treatment plants did not exist and plumbing was practically nonexistent.

Many apothecaries often provided a bottled version of the carbonated mineral waters (these products were probably produced at a local bottling plant and sold to the pharmacists.) Some bottlers labeled these bottled soda waters according to their famous "real" counterparts. Labeling bottles with the names of natural springs known to cure certain ailments—such as Vichy and Lithia—clearly indicated the types of salts and trace elements present. Other bottles were simply labeled "seltzer" or "soda."

The secrets of carbonation soon spread to the American colonies. In 1819, a pharmacist by the name of Samuel Fahnstock, of Lancaster, Pennsylvania, patented the first countertop soda water dispenser. Although others patented similar devices, he had the foresight to baptize his as a "fountain."

The soda fountain became the primary tool at the apothecary for dispensing medicinal mineral waters. Pharmacists served drinks for good health and many prescribed elixirs that could be mixed into the carbonated water. It was often necessary to add sugar syrup to this mixture to cover up the bitter "medicine" taste. It was simply a matter of time before these same pharmacists began experimenting with flavors. The resultant mixtures of tonics, sugar, and flavors became the forerunner of today's soft drinks.

Carbonated water and sweet syrup concoctions soon became a trend. Customers sought out the fountains to sample the sweet effervescent drinks. Among fountain operators, the competition for customers became fierce. To attract the masses, fountain operators invented novel flavors.

The frenzy to create the latest flavor first began when James Tufts abandoned his profitable drugstore in Somerville, Massachusetts, to cash in on his newest invention: an improved fountain that featured several syrup spigots. The setup was indeed unique. Each spigot was connected to a pipe that passed through ice that chilled the syrups before they poured from the spouts. This same cooling method produced ice-cold carbonated water.

The Commonwealth.

The Commonwealth Soda Fountain
The Commonwealth Soda Fountain was featured and sold through the A. D. Puffer & Sons catalog of Soda Water Apparatus, circa 1889. Manufactured in Boston, Massachusetts, this elaborate structure was sold at the height of the soda fountain's golden age. At the front center of the device, three spigots allowed an operator to dispense regular and carbonated water. Beneath, a row of smaller valves released an assortment of syrup flavorings into the serving glasses. At first, these grandiose units were called "fountains," but later, the term became more generalized. By the Roaring Twenties, fountain was the term used to describe the complete counter area where sodas and ice cream were served. *Collection of The New-York Historical Society*

Hires' An Uninvited Guest

Hires Root Beer was one of the first flavored soda waters available. Trade cards, like this one, first appeared on the market during the mid 1800s and were one of the ways businessmen introduced a service or product. Comprised of thin card stock, the average size of these promotional vehicles was a scant 3-by-5 inches. When the process of chromolithography was introduced, the cards bloomed with color, and by the turn of the century, trade cards were at the height of their popularity. Among all other extract makers, Hires produced the greatest amount of cards, and today, they are sought after by collectors around the world. "An Uninvited Guest" was a whimsical example of a card printed in1892. *Preziosi, Coolstock.com*

Moxie Bottles with Labels

When the Owens Automatic Bottle Machine came out in 1903, it changed the way bottlers like Moxie packaged their drinks. The new device made it possible to churn out a number of standard, inexpensive bottles at one time. Made in one piece, these containers had a molded seam that extended through the bottle top and lip. Crown cork bottle caps, invented in 1891, sealed the opening. While they are from two different time periods, the Moxie bottles shown feature the 1907 logo in raised lettering around the bottle shoulder. Paper label bottle (left) circa 1914, the applied-color label bottle (right) circa 1961. *Courtesy of Frank Potter*

In addition to his fountain, Tufts contributed many new flavors to the trade. This new line of exotic flavors made the social bar an instant success. Never before had the public tasted such tantalizing mineral water. Flavors such as wine, champagne, Peruvian beer, Maltese orange, and iced coffee with cream tempted customers. In fact, this bounty of fountain choices prompted many people to order several drinks during one visit. When it came to flavors, the sky was the limit!

Of course the social bar became more than just a place to buy a tasty beverage. Small yet palatial in their appeal, America's early soda fountains appealed to the finer senses. Here was a welcome escape from the world. Customers were drawn to the ornate decor of the first social bars. Mosaic tile floors, bar tops hewn from Italian marble, and towering ceilings, supported with marble columns, heightened the stateliness of the social bars' interiors and contributed to their feeling of fantasy. The focal point of it all was the fountain, an ornate altar to the human palate.

The soda fountain itself was often an exquisite piece of sculpture. For its day, it represented the height of design and was the definitive combination of form and function. The typical fountain often towered to a height of five feet or more. Many boasted tiered levels, each decorated with an ornate animal or god-like being. An array of spouts usually surrounded the extravagant marble base.

This man-made spring was the center of a world of wonder for everyone to enjoy. Tables and chairs were welded from the finest iron. Cushioned seats were rounded to accommodate ladies' bustles. Some fountain operators strategically placed tall ferns between tables to provide customers with a sense of privacy. By combining just the right elements, owners discovered that they could create an atmosphere that suited both youthful romance and family fun.

Competition among fountain operators was stiff and pharmacists created new products to stay in the game. Philadelphia pharmacist Charles E. Hires was a prominent example. The father of the still-popular drink known as Hires Root Beer, he launched the first national marketing campaign for a soda flavor in 1884. His attention-grabbing ads declared that Hires Root Beer was a wholesome beverage for the whole family: good for children and adults alike—even the family dog liked it!

Dr. Augustin Thompson of Lowell, Massachusetts, concocted an entirely different beverage—an invigorating nerve tonic derived from the gentian root. By 1884, Thompson modified the nerve medicine and combined it with carbonated water. He named this strong beverage "Moxie." Although its flavor was not exactly pleasing, the drink managed to survive the test of time and can still be purchased throughout New England today.

Whether fountain operators were creating drinks for medicinal purposes or for a unique taste, a wealth of flavors flooded the market. Many flavorists followed Thompson's lead and tried to concoct new formulas that combined the benefits of an elixir with carbonated water. The most promising new ingredients—the Peruvian coca leaf and the African kola

A Boost for the Soda Pop Industry

The national temperance movement of the 1800s helped reshape America's culture and create the soda fountain industry. When the Women's Christian Temperance Union was formed around 1873, women protested in front of saloons, preaching the evils of alcohol and demanding that the saloon owners close their doors. The protesters hampered businesses by standing in front of saloon entrances to block the flow of traffic, handing out leaflets, and preaching for the "purity of the home" and "temperance and morality."

Soon the temperance movement gained the support of politicians and re-ligious leaders. These groups formed a united front against what they considered to be the biggest threat to industrial society and the American home: the saloon. Saloon operators became the bane of society and many succumbed to the pressure and closed their doors forever.

In their place, social bars burst upon the American scene. Instead of selling distilled spirits, these bars specialized in ice-cold fountain drinks, such as Coca-Cola, that appealed to the entire family.

"Because Sunday is God's Day" Poster
Top, right: This poster, created by the Minnesota Good Government League and Women's Christian Temperance Union, encouraged citizens to vote "No" to the sale of alcohol on Sunday. To this day, it is illegal to sell alcohol on Sunday in the state of Minnesota. *Courtesy of the Minnesota Historical Society*

Temperance Rally, Madison, Minnesota
Above: A group of women in Madison, Minnesota, takes to the streets to protest alcohol consumption. No doubt the local saloon was nearby. *Courtesy of the Minnesota Historical Society*

nut—found their way to American shores. Both the coca leaf and the kola nut contained powerful stimulants: the alkaloids cocaine and caffeine.

Unfortunately, the patent medicine "kings" preferred to exaggerate the benefits of their magical cure-alls. And they seized upon the rumors surrounding the Peruvian coca leaf. In the 1800s, the coca leaf's reputation as a miracle plant reached such heights that it was used in almost everything from body creams to tooth powder, but was used primarily in "whole body tonics." These tonics were believed to stimulate healthy digestion, alleviate so-called female complaints, cure sexual debility, relieve depression, strengthen the blood, and provide "food" for the brain and nerves.

Henry Downes was the first to incorporate coca leaf extract into a fountain syrup and a bottled carbonated beverage. In 1881, a full seven years before Coca-Cola was trademarked, he registered the name of his drink, "Imperial Inca Coca," as a trademark. With this registration in hand, Downes was able to lay claim to the word "coca." The issue caused a heated debate. In the June 1885 issue of the *National Bottlers' Gazette,* Downes published a stern warning: The word "coca" was his and his alone. He was the first and only one to register it as part of a trademark.

Unfazed by the claim, the publication's editors responded in the July 1886 issue with a thorough tongue-lashing. They vehemently stated that the word "coca" was the name of an ingredient, and a common name could not be monopolized.

Reassured, other bottlers introduced and registered trademarks for their own versions of coca beverages, each with the word coca in its name! The first line-up of drinks included Coca-Coffee, Coca-Malta, Cocaffeine, Burgundia Coca—and of course—Coca-Cola. In a very short time span, coca beverages had established their own niche in the soft-drink industry.

Pemberton Coca-Cola Portrait

Coca-Cola inventor John Styth Pemberton was born in Knoxville, Georgia, in 1833. During his childhood the Pemberton family moved to Columbus, Georgia. In 1869, he moved to Atlanta and established himself as a druggist. Several of his compounds—including Extract of Styllinger, Gingerine, Globe Flower Cough Syrup, Indian Queen Hair Dye, Triplex Liver Pills, and French Wine of Coca—gained a loyal following. Pemberton invented Coca-Cola in May 1886 as he worked to create a new drink that would serve as a daytime "pick-me-up" for the soda fountain crowd. Unfortunately, Pemberton died on August 16, 1888, never witnessing his new beverage's rise to fame. He was buried in Columbus, Georgia. In his memory, the citizens of Columbus restored his boyhood home and built an authentic reproduction of an early apothecary. *Courtesy of The Coca-Cola Company*

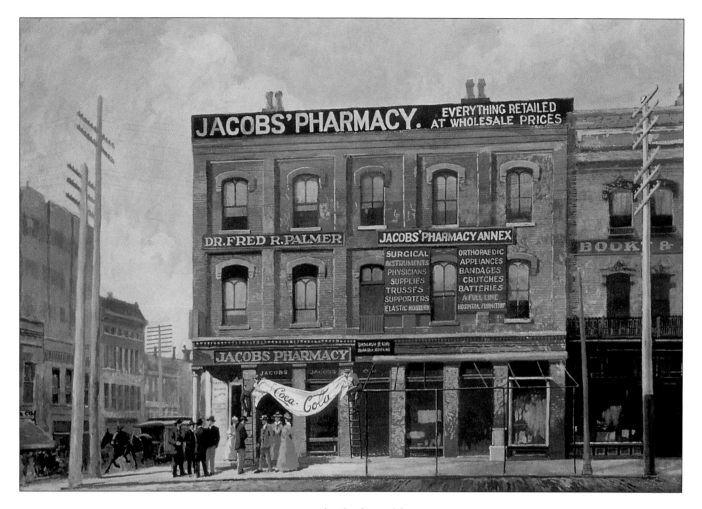

Jacobs' Pharmacy
At Jacobs' Pharmacy, the creed was "Everything Retailed at Wholesale Prices." Except perhaps, Coca-Cola. Willis Venable, the self-proclaimed "Soda Water King of the South," operated the soda fountain concession on the ground floor. There, the first glass of Coca-Cola fizzed to life in May 1886. The fountain continued to serve parched Atlanta citizens until early 1960. Later that same decade, the pharmacy was demolished to make way for a bank and office building.
Courtesy of The Coca-Cola Company

However, only the brand known as Coca-Cola contained the soon-to-be-holy combination of the coca leaf and the kola nut.

What was behind this trend and why were these ingredients so widely used? Articles in professional periodicals most likely triggered such wild enthusiasm for the kola nut. According to Milward Martin, author of *Twelve Full Ounces*, the January 1883 issue of the *American Journal of Pharmacy*, stated: "The nuts are used to form a refreshing and invigorating drink throughout a large portion of tropical Africa . . . once introduced as a beverage in civilized countries, the demand for it would soon become enormous." To the early flavormakers, this sort of hyperbole sounded more than promising. (Chemical analysis would later reveal that the kola nut contained nothing more exotic than the alkaloid caffeine!)

As it happened, a pharmacist named Dr. John Pemberton of Atlanta, Georgia, was working on a formula he hoped would create a great demand. He had achieved some success in 1885 with his French Wine of Coca formula, a nerve tonic based on the famous Vin Mariani. Angelo Françoise Mariani developed this "nutrient tonic" in 1871, and it became the rave of European society. It's not a wonder—since it was primarily a blend of sugar, red wine, and powdered coca leaf!

Because Mariani's recipe was general knowledge in the trade, there were many imitators. In 1885, shortly after the American drugmaker Parke Davis & Company debuted a replica dubbed Coca Cordial, Pemberton unveiled his own version of the drink in Atlanta. Both tonics were received with great enthusiasm. One Saturday afternoon in summer 1885, John Pemberton sold 888 bottles of French Wine of Coca. At one dollar a bottle, Pemberton raked in quite a sum of money for the time. The wine tonic continued to sell at a steady clip of two hundred to three hundred bottles a day. The sweltering summers of Atlanta called for an ice-cold pick-me-up. Pemberton's creation-in-the-making looked to be the perfect solution.

To make this new beverage, Pemberton mixed extracts of the coca leaf and the kola nut. In addition, he added a healthy dose of pharmaceutical-grade caffeine. These bitter ingredients had to be mixed with a hefty amount of sugar and natural flavorings to make them palatable. The resulting drink was a coca sensation that stood above the rest. It was most unique—and stimulating.

Fortunately, Pemberton's Atlanta was not impervious to the latest fads and amusements of the day. In 1886, it boasted five fully equipped fountains! Willis Venable, the self-proclaimed "Soda Water King of the South," operated one of these fountains. Located on the ground floor of Jacobs' Pharmacy, its twenty-five-foot marble counter was adorned with a pillared canopy of marble and stained glass. The most dominating fixture was an ornate fountain that towered to an astonishing seven feet!

And so, time and circumstance secured a place for Coca-Cola: On a warm spring day in 1886, a happy gathering of Venable's regulars sat enjoying some lively talk and liquid refreshment. Suddenly, an out-of-breath lad interrupted their conversation. Doc Pemberton had sent the youth to Venable's fountain to deliver samples of his new coca concoction.

Venable was always willing to sample new flavors. Without hesitation, he mixed the syrup with ice-cold, carbonated water and passed out free samples. At first, the customers took tentative sips. But before long they were smiling with approval. Soon the stimulating effects of the coca extract, kola nut, and caffeine rushed through their veins. No doubt, the second round elicited nothing more than the sound of hearty gulps!

IMPORTANT NOTE
REGARDING
Dangerous Substitutions.

WE CAUTION OUR PATRONS to ask for and insist on receiving "Vin Mariani." Shameful substitution is frequently attempted; the shape of our bottle and style of packing have been imitated, and even the wording of our labels and advertisements is being appropriated by unscrupulous, would-be competitors, who thus endeavor to deceive the physicians who prescribe "Vin Mariani," as well as the patients. Owing to this we are continually receiving complaints from doctors, with special requests to warn the public and the medical profession against such deceitful substitutions.

Vin Mariani Black-and-White Ad
In 1871, a shrewd Corsican named Angelo Françoise Mariani developed a "nutrient tonic" made of coca leaves and Bordeaux wine. By the 1880s, Mariani had come up with a brilliant marketing scheme. He sent gratis cases of Vin Mariani to luminaries and invited their comments. Her Royal Highness Princess of Wales, Sarah Bernhardt, John Phillip Sousa, and Jules Verne all praised the body and brain restorative. Mariani's success inspired dozens of competitors. John Pemberton's French Wine of Coca was a facsimile of Mariani's formula. The little bottles of tonic made their debut in 1885 and received an overwhelming reception in Atlanta. In 1886, Pemberton developed his first batch of a new "brain tonic" based on coca and kola. Vin Mariani ad circa 1890. *Warshaw Collection of the Smithsonian Institution*

Chapter 2

Fighting for Control of the Formula

The Beginning of the Candler Years

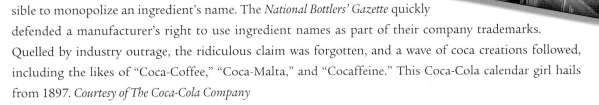

The Ideal Brain Tonic 1897 Calendar

Facing page: In 1881, coca made the dramatic leap from medicinal substance to beverage when syrup maker Henry Downes added it to a carbonated drink. An ad in the June 1884 issue of the *National Bottlers' Gazette* announced the debut: "Imperial Inca Coca, an invigorating, sparkling beverage patented and prepared only by Henry Downes, No. 402 East Twenty-Fifth Street, New York City." A year later, he registered the trademark. Armed with the documentation, Downes tried to defend exclusive right to the word "coca." But, he soon found that it was impossible to monopolize an ingredient's name. The *National Bottlers' Gazette* quickly defended a manufacturer's right to use ingredient names as part of their company trademarks. Quelled by industry outrage, the ridiculous claim was forgotten, and a wave of coca creations followed, including the likes of "Coca-Coffee," "Coca-Malta," and "Cocaffeine." This Coca-Cola calendar girl hails from 1897. *Courtesy of The Coca-Cola Company*

Inside of a Drugstore, Long Island

Right: During the early days of the 1900s, retail establishments like the Collins Pharmacy in Islip, Long Island, provided a wide range of goods and services to the public. In addition to selling film, box cameras, postcards, matches, tobacco, liquor, and other patent medicines, enterprising druggists of the day peddled a myriad of carbonated creations—Coca-Cola included. Dressed in crisp, white uniforms, the soda jerk (at the right), pharmacist (center), and retail clerk (left) were the keys to a smooth-running operation. *Library of Congress via Coolstock.com*

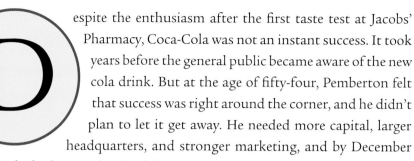

espite the enthusiasm after the first taste test at Jacobs' Pharmacy, Coca-Cola was not an instant success. It took years before the general public became aware of the new cola drink. But at the age of fifty-four, Pemberton felt that success was right around the corner, and he didn't plan to let it get away. He needed more capital, larger headquarters, and stronger marketing, and by December 1885, he had secured each of these assets.

Investors Edward Holland (the landlord of his new headquarters), Frank Mason Robinson, and David D. Doe provided the capital. Frank Robinson and David Doe were old friends from Maine who had left their home after the Civil War. Robinson and Doe owned a color printing press and intended to start an advertising agency in Atlanta.

Wooden Kegs of Coca-Cola Syrup
In the early days of Coca-Cola, Asa Candler stored syrup in used whiskey barrels. These second-hand barrels had to be clear (not charred), clean, white oak. Old gin barrels, which were coated in paraffin wax, could not be used. Eventually, the high volume of Coca-Cola sales forced Candler to use any and all barrels he could find. He developed methods for cleaning out the char, glue, and paraffin, and he had all used barrels painted bright red to hide their vulgar origin. Finally, sales grew to such proportions that the Coca-Cola Company had their own barrels made, but the tradition of painting them red continued. *Courtesy of The Coca-Cola Company*

In December 1885, Robinson and Doe made a business call to 107 Marietta Street, home of the J. S. Pemberton Company, hoping to sell some advertising services. But by the end of the meeting, Pemberton had sold the two men on his business ideas instead. Robinson and Doe agreed to join Pemberton in his business venture.

After some negotiations, all agreed that Pemberton would concentrate on manufacturing, developing, and improving patent medicines. Robinson and Doe would spearhead the print advertising campaigns. Robinson, who was trained as an accountant, would also handle the books. Edward Holland turned over the title to his property in exchange for a share in the business.

To secure the all-important capital required to operate the business, Robinson turned to his family and friends. In his book Secret Formula, Frederick Allen states that Robinson gambled everything he had on the venture. He convinced his brother Charles to invest $6,500, a sizable sum of money for that time. Robinson's father put up another $600 and two of Robinson's friends contributed $6,000.

On January 1, 1886, the Pemberton Chemical Company was formed. Holland was listed as president and J. S. Pemberton as secretary. Frank Robinson was the official bookkeeper. Shortly after the Pemberton Chemical Company took shape, Pemberton introduced the concept to both Robinson and Doe of a coca and kola flavored fountain drink. Although he was not actively involved in the business, Holland was also aware of Pemberton's business developments.

It is rumored that Frank Robinson often joined Pemberton in the basement, learning laboratory techniques and assisting with the production of medicines. And it is possible that Robinson's encouragement and keen sense of smell—essential in the development of flavorings—may have been instrumental in the creation of Coca-Cola.

Just before Pemberton Chemical Company introduced the syrup to the public, Robinson, Doe, Holland, and Pemberton met to discuss a name for their new product. It was Frank Robinson who seized the day: He combined the names of the main ingredients, dropping the "k" in kola and changing it to a "c", a strategy that gave the name "Coca-Cola" a balanced and harmonious appearance.

It can only be assumed that Holland, Robinson, and Doe looked upon Coca-Cola as a Pemberton Chemical Company product. However, Pemberton had other ideas and surreptitiously insured that no one but him would have any legal rights to the formula. In June 1887, the government issued a trademark for the Coca-Cola Syrup and Extract to John Styth Pemberton. Pemberton intentionally left Doe, Robinson, and Holland out of the deal.

Coca-Cola Dispensers

The Coca-Cola dispenser has come a long way, indeed. On the left, a modern 1950s example of a syrup dispenser—an automatic unit that mixes the carbonated water with the Coca-Cola syrup. On the right, is a completely manual 1896 ceramic syrup dispenser. Back in the good old days, pharmacy operators filled the removable bowl with syrup. Below, a metal-glass holder held the small, fluted tumbler of carbonated water. To mix the syrup and water, the fountain operator opened the brass spigot to pour the syrup into the glass. The mix ratio? It was left completely to the discretion of the operator. *Courtesy of The Coca-Cola Company*

THIS CARD ENTITLES YOU TO ONE GLASS OF

FREE Coca-Cola AT THE FOUNTAIN OF

TRADE MARK REGISTERED

ANY DISPENSER OF GENUINE COCA-COLA

Coca-Cola Coupon, Circa 1905
During the Pemberton days, Frank Robinson dreamed up these free-sample tickets for Coca-Cola as a way to introduce soda-fountain patrons to the refreshing, invigorating qualities of the drink. This "try it before you buy it" method paid off handsomely: By 1910, syrup sales to soda fountains hit 2,864,973 gallons. *Courtesy of The Coca-Cola Company*

But Pemberton's participation in the production of Coca-Cola was short-lived. In the first months of 1886, he fell seriously ill with gastroenteritis and took to his bed, incapacitated. During this time, Robinson and Doe willingly took over the reins of the day-to-day business, and proceeded in manufacturing, advertising, and distributing Coca-Cola syrup.

But the challenge of making a name for a new product was more than they had bargained for. Days and nights of hard work wore both men down. The physical strain caused tempers to flair. Despite their heroic efforts to fill a flood of orders, the two of them simply couldn't keep up with demand. And they had no money to hire additional help.

Not surprisingly, the entrepreneurs of Atlanta's fountain trade became furious when jugs of syrup arrived late or not at all. As the weeks rolled by, one fountain owner after another refused to conduct business with the Pemberton Chemical Company. By summer 1886, Coca-Cola's once promising future had fizzled. To their embarrassment, Robinson and Doe sold only twenty-five gallons of syrup! This paltry quantity of sales didn't cover the overhead costs, much less make enough to pay their salaries. Hopes dashed and deep in debt, Doe abandoned the project. He packed up the color printing press and left Atlanta in disgust.

Robinson, on the other hand, chose to stay in Atlanta. He still believed Coca-Cola could make it despite all of the early disappointments. Besides, Robinson had an emotional and financial link to the product. He was the one who gave Coca-Cola its personality when he devised the now-famous trademarked logo, a logo that had taken him months to perfect. And he had put himself on the line when he had asked both family and friends to invest sizable sums of money in the Pemberton Chemical Company and its future products. For Robinson it was a matter of pride. Coca-Cola simply had to succeed!

Pemberton entered a period of remission in 1887. During this time, he hired a crackerjack salesman by the name of Evan Walker to sell Coca-Cola syrup. Walker had a glib tongue and was capable of reeling off endless repartee. Some people said he could sell an icebox to an Eskimo. Pemberton agreed to pay Walker a sizable commission on each sale made. Working solely on this basis, Walker hit the road and began to preach the benefits of Coca-Cola to townsfolk near and far. He found a receptive market. The future of Coca-Cola looked vibrant indeed.

Meanwhile, Pemberton's health took a turn for the worse. Once again Pemberton was restricted to his bed, this time for what turned out to be the duration of his life. Pemberton tried to get his affairs in order. Most importantly, he wanted to ensure that his wife wasn't left penniless after his death. The only thing of value that he owned was the formula to Coca-Cola.

Pemberton arranged for a secret meeting with an old friend and patent medicine salesman, George Lowndes. Desperate, Pemberton asked Lowndes for financial help. Lowndes, seeing his friend in such a sorry state, couldn't refuse. As collateral, Pemberton freely offered Lowndes two-thirds interest in the Coca-Cola formula. Lowndes loaned him $1,200, and, as part of the deal, Pemberton revealed the secret formula to Lowndes.

As history records the events, Lowndes loaned the money only as a favor to a dying friend. In fact, Lowndes was busy with his own business and had no interest in Coca-Cola or its future. However, he was still a businessman who wanted to recoup his money. So, it was important that he find someone to manufacture the Coca-Cola syrup. He turned to a very likely candidate: Venable, the self-proclaimed "Soda Water King of the South."

To whet his appetite, Lowndes offered Willis Venable a hefty percentage of all Coca-Cola syrup sales. His only stipulation was that Venable produce more syrup in his spare time. Venable agreed and became Lowndes's working partner. The two moved old Doc Pemberton's crude equipment, jugs of syrup, and other ingredients from the Pemberton Chemical Company building to the basement of Jacobs' Pharmacy. Upstairs, the soda fountain would provide a visible venue for Coca-Cola.

Of course, Frank Robinson observed the proceedings with great disbelief. He stormed into Judge John Candler's office and angrily stated his case. As a favor to Robinson, the judge donned his coat and hat and made a call on Pemberton to discuss the matter in person. When Judge Candler returned, he spoke with a heavy heart: Robinson had no legal recourse! Pemberton was the sole owner of the Coca-Cola trademark.

1898 Coca-Cola Girl Calendar
Cola nuts inscribed with the words "Coca-Cola" dance around this illustrated calendar from 1898. *Courtesy of The Coca-Cola Company*

Lowndes wasn't the only one to whom Pemberton revealed the formula. Pemberton also secretly sold all the rights to the Pemberton Chemical Company (including its patent-medicine and Coca-Cola formulas) to a couple named Mayfield and their partner! Later, during a lucid moment, he admitted to the sale, but failed to return any of the cash. The Mayfield group was stuck with the original Pemberton formula with no rights to market it—at least not under the Coca-Cola name.

But the Mayfields weren't so easily dissuaded. Why not make the drink anyway and market it under another name? And so began the drink known as Chero-Cola. Rumors, innuendo, and a modest price gave Chero-Cola the boost it needed in the marketplace. Chero-Cola sold like nobody's business, and its unprecedented success eventually became a major annoyance for Candler and Coca-Cola. Since they'd purchased the Coca-Cola formula from Pemberton back in 1888, the Mayfields had divorced, and the free-spirited Mrs. Mayfield had changed her name to Diva Brown. Of course, she kept hold of the Chero-Cola Company and sent her estranged husband packing.

Coca-Cola was forced to take legal action against Diva Brown's ex-husband, Mr. Mayfield, when he started to bottle his own Coca-Cola clone called "Koke"! On November 18, 1920, the Coca-Cola Company filed legal papers in Washington, D.C. and in the four other states where Koke was sold.

The company lawyers argued that the Koke brand was marketed openly as a substitute for Coca-Cola. Their line of thinking wasn't that far off: Despite the difference in spelling, the Koke name was pronounced the same as the Coke nickname. Plus, the barrels that contained the Koke syrup were the same color red as Coca-Cola barrels! Here was an open and shut case of copyright infringement.

Unfortunately, the lower courts didn't see it that way. As it turned out, the Ninth Circuit Court of Appeals in San Francisco, California, harkened back to the Supreme Court's earlier ruling about the ambiguity of the trademark. It held that despite Mr. Mayfield's obvious trademark infringement, the Coca-Cola Company couldn't appeal to them because of its own "deceptive, false, fraudulent, and unconscionable conduct." Coca-Cola lawyers were dumbfounded by the decision.

Stockholders were just as surprised. These were hard times for Coca-Cola. The company stock fell to seventeen and seven-eighths—less than half of its value during the previous year! Investors started dumping their shares, and the stock might have plummeted even more, but there were no buyers. With its trademark in question, Coca-Cola was considered an unstable company.

The future of Coca-Cola Company fortunes—along with their trademark rights—were uncertain. On December 6, 1920, United States Supreme Court Justice Oliver Wendell Holmes handed down the decision: "The drink [Coca-Cola] characterizes the name as much as the name of the drink." Coca-Cola *was* fully entitled to trademark protection against the competing Koke brand. For the time being, Candler's company was vindicated.

With one win under its belt, Coca-Cola filed a lawsuit against the Chero-Cola Company in 1921. Diva Brown marched into the courtroom confident she had a case. She carried a document that appeared to confirm that she, her former husband, and another associate had purchased all the assets of the Pemberton Chemical Company—including the formula for Coca-Cola.

After everyone had told their story, it was no surprise that the Coca-Cola Company won the lawsuit. Pemberton's double-dealing wasn't legal and didn't hold up in court. However, Diva Brown shrugged off the judgment and continued her cola business under the new name: "Quencher." Believe it or not, this soft drink is still available in the South today.

These two cases would not be the end of imitators. As soon as the Coca-Cola Company took one copycat to court, another replaced it. To complicate matters, many of the up-and-comers claimed they had purchased the original formula from old Doc Pemberton himself! Those who hadn't met Doc Pemberton simply turned to the 1896 edition of *The Standard Formulary,* which contained a recipe for coca and cola. Although it was not the Coca-Cola formula sought after by so many, it served as a cheap and suitable imitation.

Despite the recurring cost of going to court, Candler stubbornly refused to allow others to use any portion of the Coca-Cola trademark and name. Even if an imitator's name sounded remotely similar to Coca-Cola, Candler dragged them into court. Oftentimes, Coca-Cola won, hands down. Among the trademarks that bedeviled the company lawyers were: "Cola-Ola," "Kola-Koke," "Kos-Kola," "Cola-Coke," "Chero-Cola," "Coca & Cola," "Coak," "Kaw-Lola," "Koko-Kola," "Hava-Kola," "Ko-Kola," "Co Kola," "Cola Soda," and "Klu-Ko."

Competing Cola Logos

Early studies led researchers to believe that the strange-looking kola nut contained properties similar to coca leaf. When used as the basis for a whole body tonic, pharmacists viewed the extract of the nut to be a miracle substance capable of banishing fatigue and increasing alertness. So pharmacists, who comprised the bulk of early soda fountain operators, made kola the main ingredient in many of their soda fountain creations. For Coca-Cola, this proved problematic as competing brands emerged with names that were much too similar to its own. The Coca-Cola Company fiercely defended its trademark and eventually all copycat cola creators disappeared from the scene. *Courtesy of The Coca-Cola Company*

Robinson was dumbfounded. The formula he thought belonged to the Pemberton Chemical Company belonged solely to Pemberton. And Pemberton was selling shares of interest in the Coca-Cola formula right out from under him!

In the meantime, Venable used up the existing supply of Coca-Cola syrup but neglected to make more. Cobwebs began to form on the unused gadgetry stored in Jacobs's basement. When Lowndes checked in on the operation, he was outraged. Lowndes confronted Venable and a heated argument ensued. The relationship between Lowndes and Venable quickly deteriorated into one of loathing. Now no one was making the Coca-Cola syrup!

In light of the circumstances, Lowndes decided to cut his losses and recoup what money he could. Pemberton was nearing death, and Lowndes knew that there would be no repayment of his loan. So, he offered to sell two-thirds of the Coca-Cola formula for a sum of $1,200 to Evan Walker, Pemberton's enthusiastic salesman.

Walker had a good feeling about Coca-Cola. On his extensive sales pilgrimages, he saw the sense of satisfaction that the drink elicited. As fate had it, Walker's youngest sister had just sold her home—for the exact sum of $1,200. Walker managed to smooth talk her into investing in Lowndes's proposal. She agreed to his proposal and handed over the money, despite the fact that she had no roof over her head. Walker was indeed a master salesman!

By 1887, everyone had signed on the proverbial dotted line and a relieved Lowndes had his original investment back. Walker and his sister, believing that they made the deal of a lifetime, saw great riches ahead. They hauled the collection of dusty equipment and jugs of syrup back to the Pemberton Chemical Company at 107 Marietta Street.

Meanwhile, Frank Robinson was fortunate enough to secure a job as general superintendent of Asa G. Candler & Company. Thirty-seven-year-old Asa Candler was Atlanta's wealthiest pharmacist. His business empire included a retail pharmacy, a chemical company, a manufacturing branch, and a wholesale department. The most famous of his proprietary products were Botanic Blood Balm, Delectalave (a liquid dentifrice), and Everlasting Cologne. Candler welcomed Robinson aboard as if he were a family member. But Frank Robinson never put Coca-Cola out of his mind.

Although the jugs of Coca-Cola syrup and crude manufacturing equipment gathered dust in the Pemberton Chemical Company basement and the splash that Coca-Cola had made on the fountain scene last summer was long forgotten, Robinson was determined to resurrect Coca-Cola. Perhaps part of him wanted to recoup the $13,100 he had borrowed from his brother, his father, and his friends. It's possible, too, that he wanted vindication for what he believed to be swindle. After all, Pemberton's formula

At All Soda Fountains, 1899
During this period, the Coca-Cola advertising department almost always included in their ads something on the counter containing small writing, whether it was a letter, trade card, free drink coupon, etc. Closer inspection of some of this minuscule text often revealed addresses of Coca-Cola branch offices. In 1899, Coca-Cola syrup sales topped 281,055 gallons.
Courtesy of The Coca-Cola Company

rightfully belonged to him and the other Pemberton Chemical Company partners. So Robinson turned to his friend and employer, Asa Candler.

In *Coca-Cola, An Illustrated History,* author Pat Watters quotes an Asa Candler speech from a Coca-Cola sales meeting in 1913: "One day there came along a friend of mine with a gallon of Coca-Cola. He wanted me to buy it, but not having any soda fountain, I didn't take much stock in it then. One day he suggested to me that we buy the drink and finally, some sort of way, we did get to own it. I asked him what did he expect me to do with Coca-Cola? He replied: 'See that wagon going by with all those empty beer kegs? Well we are going to push Coca-Cola until you see the wagons going by with Coca-Cola just like that.'" It is generally believed that Frank Robinson is the friend Candler mentions.

Rumor has it that it wasn't un-til Candler, who suffered from severe and chronic headaches, actually tried a glass himself, that he was convinced Coca-Cola was a worthwhile product. Candler sampled a glass of Coca-Cola at Venable's fountain and found the drink not only relieved his dyspepsia, it also banished his headache. Even *he* couldn't develop a product that provided such relief! From that point on he determined to secure the rights to Coca-Cola and market it as a headache remedy.

French Sailors on Leave, circa 1910
French sailors on leave enjoy a Coke and a smile with pretty American girls in an East Coast soda fountain.
Courtesy of The Coca-Cola Company

By 1888 Candler was in the syrup business. On April 14, 1888, Candler acquired Pemberton's remaining one-third interest to the secret formula by accepting Pemberton's share as payment on an old debt of $550 that Pemberton owed him.

After this purchase, Candler turned his attentions to Evan Walker, aware that to move ahead he had to secure the rights to the remaining ownership doled out in the previous partnerships.

Walker rejected all offers, however. It was a wise move, since Walker had everything to gain and nothing to lose by holding on to his share. But Candler didn't give up.

Eventually, the color of cash tempted Walker and his sister to relinquish their equity. Still, they sold Candler only one-half of their two-thirds share. The sale transpired April 17, 1888, when $750 changed hands. Candler would gain complete control of Coca-Cola August 30, 1888, when he handed over $1,000 to Walker and his sister for the remaining one-third.

The deal was done. Asa Candler was now sole proprietor of the Coca-Cola formula.

Chapter 3

Those Images of Innocence and Taste

Remembering the Early Days of Advertising

Coca-Cola Gal Ad, 1908

Facing Page: Although the Pure Food and Drug Act of 1906 barred the fraudulent labeling of food, this 1908 ad proclaims that Coca-Cola relieves fatigue! This may have been a reference to the effects of the caffeine in the drink, something that caused legal problems for the Coca-Cola Company. *Courtesy of The Coca-Cola Company*

Crockery Jug of Coca-Cola Syrup

Right: Selling Coca-Cola syrup was a sticky business. It was the syrup salesman's job to make sure that customers did not buy cheap, imitation cola syrups. Still, it was easy for hucksters to sway retailers since their products sold at half the cost of the Coca-Cola brand! The Coca-Cola Company incorporated multiple levels into the syrup marketing system to insure that everyone profited from the sale, and to maintain the loyalty of fountain operators. A gallon such as this one was sold to a wholesale grocer or

druggist for $1.50. That wholesaler would then sell the jugs to fountain operators for $2 a piece. Since the jug yielded one hundred glasses (sold at 5¢ each) the retailer made $3 on an initial investment of $2. *Courtesy of The Coca-Cola Company*

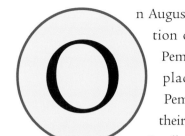

On August 16, 1888, two weeks prior to Candler's acquisition of the remaining Coca-Cola shares, John Styth Pemberton passed away. He was buried at his birthplace in Columbus, Georgia. Upon the hour of Pemberton's funeral, all of Atlanta's druggists closed their doors in his honor. Mourners descended upon Asa Candler's business office to offer their respects to a former colleague. Candler led the group in a prayer and closed with a poignant eulogy. A new era in the history of Coca-Cola had begun.

August drew to a close and the cooling breezes of September swept through Atlanta. It was late in the fountain season, which ran from May 1 to November 1. Nevertheless, Candler transported the Coca-Cola inventory from the Pemberton Chemical Company to 47 Peachtree Street, home of Asa G. Candler & Company. Since Pemberton's sale of two-thirds interest in Coca-Cola to Lowndes in July 1887, production of Coca-Cola syrup had stopped. Robinson and Candler were eager to stoke up the fire and begin cooking syrup. But before that could happen, a few improvements had to be made.

Pemberton's product had a tendency to spoil. Fountain operators were quick to point this out to Candler when he queried them about future Coca-Cola syrup purchases. Candler turned the task of stabilizing the syrup over to his chemist. Then he and Robinson tasted and sniffed their way towards an improved flavor that wouldn't spoil. With the improved syrup, the soon-to-be darling of the fountain trade was ready for its 1889 debut.

On May 1, 1889, the first Candler advertisement for Coca-Cola appeared in the *Atlanta Daily Journal.* The copy was simple, echoing the earlier advertisement by Pemberton: "Asa G. Candler & Co., Sole Proprietors of Coca-Cola. Delicious. Refreshing. Exhilarating. Invigorating. The new and popular soda fountain drink containing the tonic properties of the wonderful coca plant and the famous kola nuts. On draught at the popular soda fountains at 5 cents per glass."

The simple, understated ad worked and orders began trick-ling in. Syrup production commenced in the basement of Candler's wholesale drug business on Peachtree Street. Monday through Friday the furnace and forty-gallon copper kettle were used to manufacture Candler's Botanic Blood Balm. Saturday was syrup day. Workers cleaned out the kettle, heated up the furnace, and boiled the water and sugar, stirring the mixture with giant wooden paddles until the syrup was smooth, shiny, and thick. The trick was to keep the syrup from burning or boiling over.

Next came the sticky task of pouring hot syrup into fifty-gallon barrels. At this point in the process, Frank Robinson took over. He mixed in the crucial ingredients that rendered plain sugar syrup into Coca-Cola

Coca-Cola Calendar, 1898
The 1898 Coca-Cola calendar featured the entire year on a single printed panel. The pretty model shown here drinks serenely, quite possibly reinforcing the message that Coca-Cola "Cures Headaches" and "Relieves Mental and Physical Exhaustion."
Courtesy of The Coca-Cola Company

syrup. After the syrup had cooled, it was poured into more manageable one-gallon earthenware jugs and five-to-ten-gallon kegs. Finally workers loaded the bright red barrels and labeled jugs of syrup into a wagon and delivered the product to customers.

A trade card recalls that in 1890, syrup sales rose to 3,500 gallons, up from 2,171 in 1889. Certainly Candler's advertising strategy created higher sales. Not satisfied with selling Coca-Cola as only a refreshing beverage, Candler advertised it as both a beverage and a tonic. This strategy allowed him to market the syrup for summer and winter use, guaranteeing year-round syrup production and sales.

Candler's early sales campaigns lumped Coca-Cola with other products (particularly Delectalave), but in 1891 Candler decided to give Coca-Cola its own campaign. And what a campaign it was! A newspaper announcement reveals in succinct terms the duality of Candler's marketing strategy: "Coca-Cola. The Ideal Brain Tonic. Summer & Winter Beverage. Relieves Mental & Physical Exhaustion. Specific for Headache." Coca-Cola was an amazing product—it could provide so much relief for such a small cost!

Candler took this campaign one step further by soliciting personal endorsements from respected members of Atlanta society. According to Lawrence Dietz, author of *Soda Pop,* a quote from Doctor Robert W. Westmoreland of Atlanta was featured in a Coca-Cola ad: "From a knowledge of the medicinal agents comprising the formula of Coca-Cola, together with a personal experience of its effects, I feel safe in recommending the preparation as an agreeable tonic, a pleasant and refreshing beverage, while its efficacy as a remedy for nervous headache will commend it to those suffering from that malady." As if that weren't enough, another physician, Doctor C. A. Stiles (also of Atlanta) recommended drinking Coca-Cola for a variety of ailments ranging from biliousness to voice strain. Even a librarian at the State Library of Georgia recommended it as a cure for nervous depression and overexcitement, topping the endorsement with: "I believe it to be good for indigestion." Who could resist such hype? The public responded by gulping down an astonishing 668,000 glasses in 1891.

It is not surprising that this success prompted Asa Candler to rethink his role in the future of Coca-Cola. And so Candler set out to make Coca-Cola the primary purpose of his business. He sold his other business interests and closed out his entire inventory, using the money to reinvest

Coca-Cola Service to the Carriage, 1906
Back during the days when Coca-Cola was still sold for a nickel a glass and women did their shopping by horse-drawn carriage, enterprising city fountain operators served shoppers in the comfort of their surreys. This 1906 iteration of "curb service" was the ultimate in convenience and service: Customers just pulled up to the curb, gave the fountain boy an order, and waited. With service like that, who needs a drive-thru window? This ad appeared on the back cover of the May 1906 issue of the *Housekeeper. Courtesy of The Coca-Cola Company*

Early Coca-Cola Bottling Shed
Many small bottling operations continued using old equipment until the crown stopper was adopted. Forced to update their bottle-filling machinery, a good number cut corners in other departments. While this 1914 bottler sports an updated filling table, the bottling works is conducted in a converted barn. What's more, the "bottle washing" department relies on an old hand-cranked soak and wash machine. *Courtesy of The Coca-Cola Company*

in Coca-Cola. In the later part of 1891, Candler moved the Coca-Cola operation to the second and third floors of 42½ Decatur Street. Shortly after that, Candler filed for a petition to incorporate The Coca-Cola Company.

The government granted the charter on January 29, 1892. Asa Candler, F. W. Prescott, J. M. Berry, John S. Candler, and Frank M. Robinson were elected as directors of the Coca-Cola Company, a Georgia-based corporation. Candler was elected president, John S. Candler vice-president, and Frank Robinson became secretary. One thousand shares of stock were issued, with a par value of one hundred dollars each. Asa Candler purchased five hundred shares and, as a fitting tribute for the work and effort that Frank Robinson had bestowed upon Coca-Cola, transferred ten shares to him. It was official: Coca-Cola was now a part of corporate America.

This early success of Coca-Cola was in part due to the enthusiastic salesmanship of Samuel Candler Dobbs. Dobbs was the son of one of Asa Candler's older sisters and had grown up in a one-room shack near the Alabama state line. He had six months of formal education under his belt and believed that the happiest day of his life was when his uncle Asa became president of the Coca-Cola Company.

The gangly seventeen-year-old had arrived in Atlanta in 1886, willing to do anything for room and board. Candler handed him a broom. Undaunted, young Dobbs accepted his entry-level position. When his Uncle Asa began manufacturing Coca-Cola syrup, Dobbs reveled. He was in paradise—Coca-Cola paradise! As it turned out, Coca-Cola was his favorite beverage, and he could literally drink it by the gallon if he had the time. Suddenly he was allowed to indulge himself whenever he wanted, and he did, drinking up to fifteen glasses of Coca-Cola a day!

Of course, Candler realized that anyone who possessed such an unabashed enthusiasm for a product would make an ideal candidate for selling it. It wasn't long before Candler rethought Dobbs's position and took back the broom. In 1889, Samuel Dobbs became a route salesman for Coca-Cola. He and three other salesmen—G. W. Little, J. W. Philips, and Daniel Bevill Candler—were the first syrup salesmen for the fledgling organization. This was new territory! There were no guidelines to follow, and no proven strategy for closing the sale. They would invent them all.

The sales territory, which included Georgia and the other states of the South, was vast for the time. In those days, travel by horse or train, covering such a large area, proved to be an awesome task. But this didn't hinder Dobbs. He gladly traveled by rail and stagecoach, taking two fountain seasons to cover the territory outlined by his uncle. Dobbs headed as far west as the Mississippi River and as far north as North Carolina, extolling the enticing qualities of Coca-Cola everywhere.

In 1891, Dobbs retired his sales bag and returned to corporate life in Atlanta. Instead of praising his nephew for his hard work and a job well done, Asa reprimanded Dobbs for selling syrup to back-alley bottlers. As a salesman Dobbs believed that a sale was a sale, regardless of who purchased the syrup. Candler strongly disagreed. The self-professed bottlers to whom Dobbs had sold syrup were often located in rural areas where they set up shop in or behind a barn. Their equipment consisted of a secondhand bottling table and discarded Hutchinson bottles. Few bothered to wash out the troublesome Hutchinson bottles with their annoying spring stoppers. Bottling could be a primitive and thoroughly unsanitary affair. And Candler issued a stern warning to all his salesmen: Keep away from the disreputable bottler.

In his book *Secret Formula,* Frederick Allen recounts that Candler reprimanded his nephew by telling him: "There are too many folks who are not responsible, who care nothing about the reputation of what they put up, and I am afraid the name [of Coca-Cola] will be injured." Dobbs realized that bottling had a long way to go, but he also saw the limitations of selling exclusively to soda fountains—there were only so many soda fountains to pitch to. The bottled beverage could be sold in more ways, to more markets.

Even though the two disagreed about various issues of bottling and the soda fountains, Candler did acknowledge his nephew's success. During his on-the-road training, Dobbs had become a man. Still, he needed a bit more polish. Candler arranged for a tutor to round out his nephew's

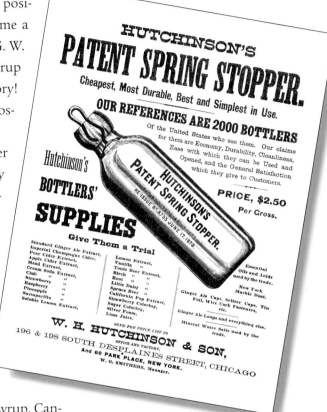

Hutchinson's Patent Spring Stopper
A plethora of internal stoppers flooded the market by the late 1800s, but one rose to dominate the field: the simple and economical design patented by Charles G. Hutchinson of Chicago, Illinois, on April 8, 1879. The clever design permitted the bottle to be opened by pushing the stem into the bottleneck while the wire loop prevented the stem from falling back into the bottle. Pulling up on the stem forced the rubber disk to block the bottle's top, closing the bottle. *Courtesy of John R. Paul*

education. At the same time, he gave Dobbs a desk job in Atlanta, allowing him to work by day and study by night. Eventually, Asa promoted Dobbs to supervisor of the shipping department. There was one caveat: Any mistakes would be subtracted directly from his paycheck!

Candler hired a small army of salesmen to blanket the Midwest, a previously untapped market. When the sales force marched into the new territory, they discovered that it was a difficult region to crack. The Midwesterners were a skeptical group. They had never heard of this peculiar southern drink called Coca-Cola! The majority of them were hard-working farmers and invariably, they poured every cent they earned back into their farms. They had no intention of spending their hard-earned cash on something as frivolous as a fountain drink!

As the sales force chipped away at the skeptics, Dobbs completed his education. He was soon ready to fly on his own. Frank Robinson took Dobbs under his wing and tutored him in every aspect of the business, including purchasing ingredients, manufacturing syrup, and outfitting salesmen with advertising materials.

But Dobbs wanted more. His secret ambition was to have Robinson's job as supervisor of the Coca-Cola advertising department. Dobbs dreamed of devising and implementing new ways to promote Coca-Cola. Before long, Dobbs was bombarding Robinson with all sorts of suggestions. Some were pretty good. Soon thereafter, the two began working as a team.

After some careful thought, Dobbs and Robinson decided to revisit the free sampling campaign. But this time, they added a new twist: Instead of mailing the coupons to customers, salesmen distributed thousands of coupons directly to the fountain operators. And these coupons were good for a free Coke for the customer and a friend. This two-in-one offer was well received by the public. After all, who wouldn't enjoy a free, refreshing beverage with a friend?

The pair also recruited Ed Grant, an independent sign painter in Atlanta, to design an oilcloth banner. The execution was flawless! In bright red paint, the Coca-Cola trademark appeared to jump out from the white background. The slogan "Delicious and Refreshing" appeared in tranquil blue. Wowed by the effect, Dobbs and Robinson set a goal: Thousands of these banners were to be placed on drugstore awnings nationwide. Within

Baird's Coca-Cola Clock
Coca-Cola offered the Chicago-era Baird Clock with an eight-day movement, manufactured between 1896 and 1900, as a premium for high-volume dealers of Coca-Cola syrup. It's a curious promotional item, as it reflects the ambivalence that Coca-Cola portrayed in some of its early advertising: While it extols a refreshing beverage with one slogan, another cites its use as a headache and nerve tonic.
Courtesy of The Coca-Cola Company

1901 Flowers Motif Calendar

In 1901, Coca-Cola syrup sales topped 370,877 gallons. This calendar, printed by Wolfe & Company of Philadelphia, Pennsylvania, promoted the Chicago, Illinois; Philadelphia, Pennsylvania; Los Angeles, California; and Dallas, Texas branch offices.

Courtesy of The Coca-Cola Company

the year, the banners began to appear all over America, capturing the attention of passersby and bringing public awareness of Coca-Cola to new heights.

Dobbs and Robinson also increased the sales by offering dealer incentives—rewards to fountain operators who had big volume sales. Top producers received items such as ceramic syrup urns, metal signs, posters, change trays, serving trays, wall clocks, and decals, all emblazoned with the red-and-white Coca-Cola trademark and a catchy slogan.

Not only were the items practical, they added to the soda fountain's ambiance. Best of all, they sold product. The more Coca-Cola items there were at the soda fountain to look at, the better. When a fountain customer was surrounded by the Coca-Cola name, it was difficult to avoid ordering anything but a glass of Coca-Cola—whether they had planned to or not! And so began a completely new method of marketing: impulse buying.

Robinson and Dobbs capitalized on other buying impulses, too. In 1892 they launched what was later dubbed the "pretty girl" calendar—a Coca-Cola calendar adorned with a femme fatale. By this time the technology of color lithography had made great strides forward, enabling printers to produce large quantities of full-color graphic art at a reasonable price.

Since 1892 the Coca-Cola Company has issued a new calendar every year. At one time, Coca-Cola's eye-catching calendars were so popular that on every New Year's Day, customers flocked to their local fountain to see the latest one. Fans of Coca-Cola and the pretty girl calendar gathered around to inspect the new edition, give their nod of approval, and order a Coke.

The team of Robinson and Dobbs never tired of devising new ways to promote Coca-Cola. Office buildings provided them with a vast, untapped territory, and soon, they had teams of salesmen visiting the bastions of the business world. At the beginning of each day, every salesman received a caseload of promotional items, including ink blotters, fans, paperweights, and calendars. The rule was that every item had to be given away and no one was allowed to return with leftover freebies. Coca-Cola salesmen found themselves in the best physical shape of their lives, as traipsing up and down stairs and popping into offices proved quite a workout.

Japanese fans became a huge hit with women. Like the calendars, they were one of Coca-Cola's most ingenious marketing strategies. One side of the fan featured a scene, while the other side presented the words "Coca-Cola." As a lady fanned herself, the words fluttered either directly at her or at any onlookers. It was the perfect form of subliminal advertising.

Victorian Girl Coca-Cola Tray
This 1898 vintage "Victorian Girl" Coca-Cola serving tray—the oldest of its kind known to exist—is a graphic example of the demure themes Coca-Cola employed during the early years (note what appears to be a coupon on the table). During the year that this tray was issued, fountains in Canada; Honolulu, Hawaii; and Mexico served Coke. By December 13, 1898, the Coca-Cola Company moved into its new headquarters at Edgewood and College Avenues. The building was three stories high and shaped like a generous wedge of pie. Although the triangle-shaped structure was designed to house the growing needs of the booming company, within ten years it had become too cramped and the Coca-Cola Company moved once again. *Courtesy of The Coca-Cola Company*

Coca-Cola Ghost Sign

By 1894, Robinson and Dobbs had commissioned artist Jim Couden to paint the first wall sign in Cartersville, Georgia. Soon, more than twenty thousand Coca-Cola wall signs colored the American landscape in red and white. The ubiquitous "wall as sign" strategy created a national awareness of Coca-Cola. Brand-name marketing was in its infancy, and Coca-Cola was at the forefront of creating public awareness of brand image. Wall signs were part of Coca-Cola's marketing strategy until the 1950s. Today, many of these "ghost signs" are uncovered during renovations and remodeling, revealing a window that looks back into America's past. *©2001 Mike Witzel, Coolstock.com*

1910 Happy Days Calendar
Another very rare calendar highly prized by collectors, the 1910 "Happy Days" calendar capitalized on the exuberance of the times. Between 1910 and 1916, the Coca-Cola Company cashed in on this giddiness, spending $11 million on advertising.
Courtesy of The Coca-Cola Company

By 1894, Robinson and Dobbs had commissioned artist Jim Couden to paint the first wall sign in Cartersville, Georgia. Soon, more than twenty thousand Coca-Cola wall signs colored the American landscape in red and white. The ubiquitous "wall as sign" strategy created a national awareness of Coca-Cola. Dobbs and Robinson hatched a plan to paint Coca-Cola signs on every barn in the tough-to-crack Midwestern market. Of course, the farmers were compensated handsomely. With Coca-Cola staring them in the face at every turn, residents didn't know what hit them. It took a lot of effort, but Midwesterners, who once raised eyebrows at Coca-Cola, were fast becoming addicts!

Despite these many successes, Robinson and Dobbs would soon relinquish their advertising domain to the professionals. As the 1800s drew to a close, the pundits of the new century pronounced everything previously known as being "outdated." The tried-and-true methods of advertising were discarded and new methods were ushered in. Instead of dreaming up their own ads, companies seriously interested in reaching a national audience hired advertising agencies.

At the dawn of the twentieth century, soda fountains, also, were becoming a thing of the past. The advent of the automobile changed the pace of life in America. People no longer wanted to sit at soda fountain counters and leisurely sip soda. They wanted to drive around with a bottle of Coca-Cola instead.

Without looking back, America's advertising gurus replaced the familiar glass of Coca-Cola with a shapely, portable, glass bottle. With the top popped on the future, Coca-Cola was well on its way to becoming an American icon.

Tray with Girl in Bonnet, 1914
Known as "Betty," this Coca-Cola model appeared on trays, pocket mirrors, signs, posters, calendars, and other promotional items. From an advertising standpoint, one of the best ways to promote brand-name recognition was to serve Coca-Cola on metal serving trays. The tray, with a pleasant visual and stylized logo, mirrored the product. This tray also came in a smaller version. *Courtesy of The Coca-Cola Company*

Chapter 4

From Syrup Jug to Soda Pop Bottle

Birth of the Bottling Industry

Coca-Cola Service to the Car

Facing page: By the time the horse-drawn carriage was replaced by the motorcar, the idea of grabbing a glass of Coca-Cola "on the go" was firmly planted. Sightseeing patrons whizzing about in their smoking, sputtering automobiles liked nothing better than to pull into a roadside restaurant and be served in their seats. Eateries accommodated the demand for in-car service, and before too long, the drive-in restaurant that catered to patrons in their cars was born. *Courtesy of The Coca-Cola Company*

Early Coca-Cola Delivery Truck

Right: During the early heyday of advertising, the Coca-Cola Sales and Advertising Department relied on representatives in horseless machines to traverse the countryside and spread the good news of Coca-Cola. Armed with a full load of advertising banners, die-cut point-of-purchase displays, posters, fans, and every other type of promotional item that you could imagine, these intrepid hucksters pioneered the modern advertising methods taken for granted today. *Courtesy of The Coca-Cola Company*

Coca-Cola's popularity was the result of careful advertising, promotion, *and* shrewd sales deals. With profits possible for all players, Asa Candler positioned Coca-Cola to be the star of the trade. The high volume of Coca-Cola syrup sales was directly related to a generous three-tier sales plan. Coca-Cola had a simple strategy that insured profits at every sales level, particularly for the fountain operator. To give the sales force the inspiration to sell more syrup, the profits for each level were protected by a strict policy: No fountain operator could buy syrup directly from the Coca-Cola Company.

Here's how the plan worked: The Coca-Cola Company governed the first tier. It sold syrup to a wholesaler, or jobber, for a $1.50 for every one-gallon jug. This jobber handled the second tier of operations and sold the one-gallon Coca-Cola jug for $2.00, earning a fifty-cent-per-gallon profit. His job was to sell syrup to retailers who, in turn, sold soda water to the customer.

The highest profits were offered at the third tier, the level held by the soda-fountain proprietor. Here, a one-gallon jug of concentrated Coca-Cola syrup yielded approximately one hundred glasses (when it was properly diluted with carbonated water). Considering that each glass sold for a nickel, proprietors gained substantial returns. A fastidious and customer-savvy fountain operator could make a three-dollar profit for every gallon of Coca-Cola syrup consumed—a hefty profit margin in those days.

Unfortunately, the soda fountain money-machine didn't last forever. Sit-down fountains created such a big market for drinks like Coca-Cola

Predecessors of the Crown Closure
Predecessors of the crown closure are: (first row, left to right) cork, cork fastener of 1857, Matthews gravitating stopper of 1865, Codd Ball Stopper of 1873. (Second row, left to right) Lightning stopper of 1875, Hutchinson stopper of 1879, Klee stopper of 1880, Bernadin bottle cap of 1885. (Third row, left to right) Joly stopper of 1885, Twitchell floating ball stopper of 1885, bottle seal of 1885, Crown cap of 1892. *Reprinted with permission, National Soft Drink Association*

Assortment of Schweppes Bottles

Among the numerous shapes, sizes, and configuration of bottles once used by J. Schweppe and Company, the clay and green glass egg-shaped bottles (pictured in the foreground) are the most famous. These crude containers, used in the early days of soda bottling, date from 1809. Note that while the company was named after Jacob Schweppe, it typically referred to its product as "Schweppes." *Courtesy of Cadbury Schweppes p.l.c.*

Hutchinson Blob Top Bottle

Above, left: One challenge soft drink bottlers grappled with early on was the search for the perfect stopper. This bottle, the Hutchinson Blob Top Bottle, was designed to accommodate the Hutchinson Stopper, which featured a wire loop and rubber disk that rested inside the bottle's neck. With the invention of the stopper, bottle manufacturers designed a bottle with a thick, rounded top and a short, stout neck capable of withstanding the pressure exerted during the insertion process and filling operation (the Hutchinson stopper was inserted into the bottle after the bottle was filled). Both the design of the bottle and the design of the stopper dictated that the bottles be filled by hand. From 1885 to 1910, blob top bottles such as this one were used (with rare exception) exclusively for soda pop. Collectors refer to them as the "Hutchinson blob," and they came in several styles and sizes. Some sported fluted bottoms, some rare ones featured paneled sides. These bottles varied in size from six-and-one-half ounces to eight ounces. Most Hutchinson blobs came in some shade of green, although manufacturers did offer amber, cobalt blue, and clear varieties. *Courtesy of the Coca-Cola Company*

Johnson Crown Bottle Cap Machine

Above, right: William Painter's small, metal cap with cork liner and ribbed skirt revolutionized the bottle industry. The Baltimore, Maryland, resident began working on the new closure in 1889. The original cap featured an exaggerated, long skirt with deeply crimped depressions. A loop attached to the cap (this was before the invention of the bottle opener and twist-off cap) helped soda drinkers remove the cap. This loop gave the cap the appearance of a miniature crown, a term so appropriate that eventually, it became the generic name for all such caps. Improved versions of the cap hit the market in 1890, and again in 1891. On February 2, 1892, the government issued patents to William Painter for all three versions. With these patents in hand, Painter rolled out a new capping machine. On April 1, 1892, the Crown Cork and Seal Company was organized as a stock company, capitalized at $1,000,000. Crown Cork and Seal is still in operation today. *Courtesy of the Dr Pepper Museum, Waco, Texas*

that consumers wanted more. People "on the go" soon demanded a portable beverage that they could take with them. Fortunately, a "to go" method of soothing parched throats was already in the works. With a new container, venue, and attitude, refreshment in a bottle was the future.

It was at about this time that Joseph Biedenharn of Vicksburg, Mississippi, began his bottling career. Biedenharn was the first to bottle Coca-Cola, an event that changed life forever for him and his family. Six of his seven brothers also eventually went into the Coca-Cola bottling business. Joseph remained an enthusiastic Coca-Cola bottler for fifty-eight years. In the early days of soda water, H. H. Biedenharn and Son operated a combination mini-mart, lunch counter, bakery, and soda fountain. It was a place where people of all backgrounds could sit down, side by side, and enjoy a twelve-ounce glass of Coca-Cola with a homemade jellyroll or a slice of pound cake. In a 1965 interview featured in *Coca-Cola Heritage* by P. Randolph Mayo, Jr., Joseph's brother Albert Biedenharn explained: "We sold a half-pound slice of cake for a nickel, a twelve-ounce glass of Coca-Cola for a nickel and people came from all over town to eat lunch down there." With generous portions, tasty drinks, and low prices, Biedenharn's operation provided everything that local customers wanted.

Albert, who was only nine at the time, was working in Joseph's store as a soda skeet when Joseph Biedenharn began his bottling business. As he tells it: "Joe was selling candy and cakes and knickknacks and stuff like that. They [customers] wanted him to ship them soda water. He would take orders for a lot of soda water. He would turn it over to another bottler there [in Vicksburg] and this bottler disappointed his customers one Fourth of July holiday, after they had 'laid the crops by'—so our customers got mad at us. Joe said that if he was going to take orders for soda water, he might as well be in the business [of bottling], so he sent to Chicago (he had connections up there), and he found a lot of junk bottles, and he got himself a Hutchinson syrup pump and filler, and he just sawed two Coca-Cola barrels in two as a washer—and he was in business. He already had the CO_2 [for his soda fountain]."

Within thirty days Biedenharn was up and running—bottling lemon-, strawberry-, and sarsaparilla-flavored soda pop. Unlike some of his counterparts, he considered Coca-Cola syrup too expensive a commodity to put in a ten- or twelve-ounce bottle to be sold at fifty cents a case. But he soon changed his mind. By 1894, customer demand for bottled Coke increased, and he began filling special orders (he sold Coke by the bottle, not by the case). Up until that time, Joseph Biedenharn was happily wholesaling Coca-Cola syrup to other soda fountains in the Vicksburg area. Now he was in the business of bottling it.

Biedenharn already had the perfect outlet in place to distribute bottled Coca-Cola. He had a combined form of "fast food" service and a grocery delivery service underway. The operation consisted of four men with mule-driven wagons. As the mules clip-clopped over the dirt roads,

Hutchinson's Patented Spring Stopper
A plethora of internal stoppers flooded the market by the late 1800s. The simple and economical design patented by Charles G. Hutchinson of Chicago, Illinois, on April 8, 1879, became one of the more popular stoppers. His design featured a loop of heavy wire and a stopper gasket. The thick wire protruded above the bottle's neck and acted like a spring. The gasket extended through the neck and down into the bottle. After filling the bottle with soda pop, bottlers pulled the gasket up by the wire to seal the bottle. To open the bottle, soda pop drinkers gave the stopper a swift slap with the palm of the hand. When the gasket plunged through the neck and down into the bottle, the pressure release created a distinct "pop" sound, and that's how carbonated drinks came to be known as soda pop!
Courtesy of The Coca-Cola Company

THE Coca-Cola BOTTLER

OFFICIAL ORGAN OF THE COCA-COLA BOTTLERS' ASSOCIATION

GOLDEN ANNIVERSARY OF THE BOTTLING OF COCA-COLA
1894 1944

August 1944

Bottler Joseph Biedenharn

Joseph August Biedenharn of Vicksburg, Mississippi, was the first to bottle Coca-Cola. In 1890, Samuel Candler Dobbs (the nephew of Asa Candler and a Coca-Cola salesman) persuaded Biedenharn to purchase his first five-gallon jug of Coca-Cola syrup. As it turns out, it was a fortuitous event. The Biedenharn soda fountain purchased so much syrup that even Asa Candler was impressed. At Candler's invitation Biedenharn became a jobber, wholesaling the syrup to other Vicksburg area fountains. Four years later Biedenharn began bottling Coca-Cola. The first two cases of bottled Coca-Cola were shipped to Asa Candler in Atlanta, who responded that "it was fine." For the next three years Biedenharn was the only bottler of Coca-Cola. Then, in 1897, the Valdosta Bottling Works of Valdosta, Georgia, started a limited production of bottled Coca-Cola.

the drivers called out a list of their wares in a rhythmic tone. The rumbling wagons contained everything from sandwiches to pies to groceries to bottled soda water. Before too long, Biedenharn made sure that the drivers loaded their wagons with cases of bottled Coca-Cola.

Naturally, the Coca-Cola Company did not officially sanction these unorthodox operations. However, Asa Candler was well aware of Biedenharn's enterprise since the first two cases of bottled Coca-Cola were shipped directly to him in Atlanta, Georgia. According to Biedenharn, Candler acknowledged the receipt of the bottled Coca-Cola with a note saying: "It was fine." However, Candler never did return the bottles!

It was a well-known fact that Asa Candler viewed the bottling business with a twitch of skepticism. For him, the idea of bottling was just a passing phase—one that could not possibly endure. There were just too many problems with the fledgling industry, including sanitation, distribution, and bottle and closure design. But Biedenharn wouldn't let minor matters stop him. He forged ahead, expanding his bottling business until it included areas outside of Vicksburg, Mississippi. Through trial and error, the newborn bottling industry overcame all of these obstacles.

While Biedenharn was busy bottling Coca-Cola, lawyers Benjamin Franklin Thomas, Joseph Brown Whitehead, and John Thomas Lupton were working to establish the foundation of the Coca-Cola bottling industry.

On July 19, 1899, Thomas and Whitehead approached Asa Candler with the idea of placing Coca-Cola in a bottle. Candler was staunchly against their ideas, and he fervently attempted to dissuade the young men from following through with their plans. He was certain he wanted nothing to do with such an enterprise. It was not until they repeatedly reassured Candler that they would assume full responsibility for the venture that Candler reluctantly gave in. According to Pat Watters, author of *Coca-Cola: An Illustrated History*, Candler told the pair: "If you boys fail in the undertaking, don't come back to cry on my shoulder, because I have very little confidence in this bottling business."

They worked out an agreement that gave Thomas and Whitehead the exclusive rights to bottle Coca-Cola everywhere in the United States except New England, part of Texas, and Mississippi. Candler excluded New England because an earlier contract with Seth W. Fowle & Sons of Boston was still in effect. He omitted Texas because another contract was in the works with a Corsican, Texas, businessman (the deal never materialized). Mississippi was also held back because Candler wanted to honor Joseph

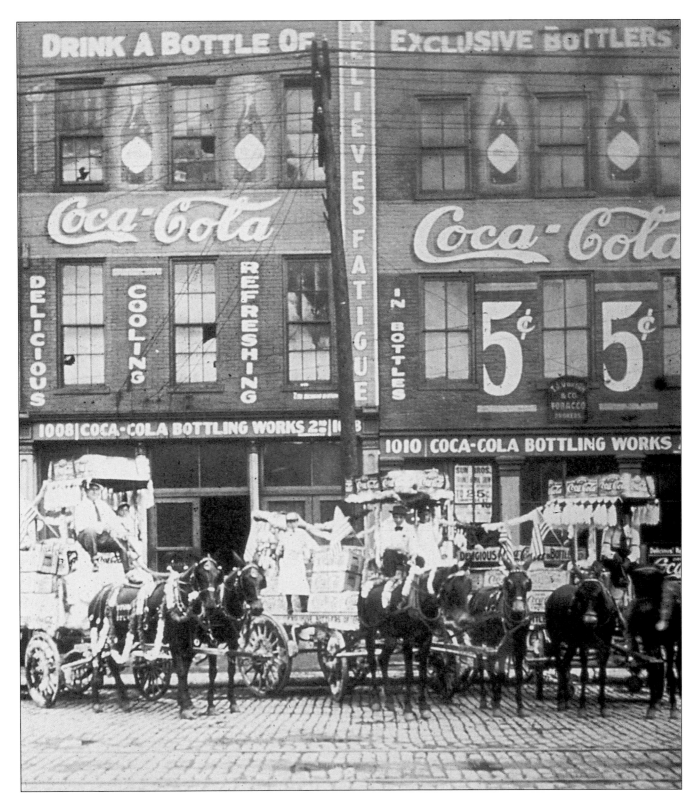

Coca-Cola Bottling Works

With deliveries made by horse-drawn cart, the Coca-Cola Bottling Works was one of the early bottlers of the brand. Located in city districts where warehouse space was cheap and there was room to grow, many such bottlers sprang up across the country to package and distribute product. Note the straight-sided Coca-Cola bottle depicted on the façade. *Courtesy of The Coca-Cola Company*

Those Famous Curves

At the Atlanta convention, many Coca-Cola bottlers expressed concerns to the Coca-Cola Company about the size, shape, and label of the 1900s bottle. At the time, merchants chilled bottles of pop in large tubs of ice water. Customers had to roll up their sleeves and reach into the icy water to grab a bottle. Oftentimes, the dripping bottle emerged without a label. While soaking in the water, the labels became unglued and slid to the bottom of the tub. What could be done to insure that customers knew they held a bottle of Coca-Cola in their hands?

The bottlers put their heads together and decided that they needed to trademark a unique bottle that was just a bit smaller than the standard eight ounces. A bottle unique to Coca-Cola would encourage brand-name recognition. And the slightly smaller bottle, sold at the same price, would increase profits. The Coca-Cola bottlers challenged bottle manufacturers to a contest to create this one-of-a-kind bottle—one that customers would recognize even when they held it in the dark. The contest winner would hold the patent and receive royalties on all the bottles manufactured, whether the bottles were produced by their company or by another.

The bottlers formed a committee to pick the winning entry and set the deadline for early 1916. Only ten bottle-makers entered the competition. The bottle designed by Root Glass Company of Terre Haute, Indiana, won hands-down.

As the story goes, the summer of 1913 was so hot that the Root Glass Company closed down its plant. This gave owner C. J. Root the opportunity to concentrate on creating a new design for Coca-Cola. To get things started, plant superintendent Alex Samuelson instructed the company's accountant, T. Clyde Edwards, to obtain all the information he could on the coca bean and the kola nut.

Samuelson returned with a detailed line drawing of what he thought was the coca bean. But instead of retrieving a drawing showing the coca bean, Samuelson had found one of the cocoa bean! Call it fate, luck, or chance, that simple mistake resulted in the famous green-tinted bottle with those familiar curves we know today. The prototypes produced by shop supervisor, Earl Dean, captured the image of the curvaceous bean right down to its distinctive ridges.

Unfortunately, these prototypes were too voluptuous for the standard bottling equipment of the day. With a little trimming, a slimmer version of the original designs emerged, the bottle's basic curves and ridges still intact. The Root bottle was so distinctive that that the leading designers of the day lauded it as "the most perfectly designed package in use." In 1960, the design became the first soda pop bottle to have a recognized trademark registered with the U.S. Patent Office. Modern Coke bottles, although they're made of plastic, maintain the same curvaceous, ridged look that says Coca-Cola.

Early Coca-Cola Curves Fat Bottle
In the summer of 1913 the Root Glass Company of Terre Haute, Indiana, prepared to enter a bottle design competition sponsored by Coca-Cola bottlers. Seeking inspiration for a unique design, plant superintendent Alex Samuelson sent a company accountant to the library to find information on the coca bean and kola nut. He returned with an intricate line drawing of what he thought was the coca bean. But it was a mistake: The picture actually showed a cocoa bean! The happy accident was this bulbous version of the familiar Coke container.
Courtesy of The Coca-Cola Company

| 1894 | 1899–1902 | 1900 —— 1916 | 1915 | 1923 | 1937 | 1957 | 1961 | 1975 |

Packaging Chronology

Above: From the 1894 Biedenharn Candy Company Hutchinson-style stopper bottle to the 1975 one-way plastic bottle (if you can call it that), the Coca-Cola container has gone through numerous iterations. Joseph A. Biedenharn of Vicksburg, Mississippi, was the first bottler of Coca-Cola. *Courtesy of The Coca-Cola Company*

Root Glass Company Bottle

Right: Root's mold shop supervisor Earl Dean produced a number of prototypes based on the cocoa bean drawing. But the stylish curves and ridges of the design proved too voluptuous for the standard bottling equipment of the day, so the prototypes were rejected. Only two of these original Dean prototype bottles are known to exist today; one resides at the archives of the Coca-Cola Company. The design (a modified version) was patented in Alex Samuelson's name on November 16, 1915. *Courtesy of The Coca-Cola Company*

Coca-Cola Bottle

Bottom: The overly exaggerated Mae West design produced by the Root Glass Company never made it to the store shelves. Coca-Cola settled on the more stream-lined, svelte design shown here—a model that was a lot easier to hold in one hand. Over the years, thirsty customers picked up hundreds of millions of these bottles (affectionately nicknamed hobble-skirt bottles by collectors). Although the design was patented in 1915, it was not until 1920 that all Coca-Cola bottlers used the contoured bottle. The reason for the delay was simple economics: Since bottlers had a large supply of straight-side bottles in their inventory, they delayed switching to the new design until after they'd depleted their inventory. Many bottlers may have produced Coca-Cola in both the curved and straight-side bottle during the same period. *Courtesy of The Coca-Cola Company*

Coca-Cola Bottle Wagon
Local bottlers like this Shreveport, Louisiana, outfit were proud of their Coca-Cola product—and rightly so. During the early 1900s, the horseless carriage provided the perfect means to get the word out, even if that meant installing an oversized billboard on one of your delivery wagons and driving it around town. *Courtesy of The Coca-Cola Company*

Biedenharn's right to that territory. The men signed the six-hundred-word contract on July 21, 1899, and Thomas and Whitehead walked away with the bottling rights to practically every state in the Union. The price for these rights was one dollar, which was never collected!

Thomas and Whitehead had only to devise a way to franchise this vast territory to would-be bottlers. While Thomas had five thousand dollars to open a factory, Whitehead did not. So, Whitehead turned to John Lupton who purchased half of the interest in Whitehead's contract with the Coca-Cola Company. Then he too opened a bottling plant. Thomas opened his plant in late fall 1899 in Chattanooga, Tennessee. One year later, the Whitehead/Lupton plant opened in Atlanta, Georgia.

Now the vast expanse of America was theirs for the taking. Unfortunately, bottling a beverage and selling it nationwide was a daunting task that required stamina, fortitude, and a whole lot of cash. The two young men possessed the vision, but they lacked the capital. They began to seek others to invest in this ground-floor opportunity.

But Thomas and Whitehead disagreed on the terms of the investment agreements. Thomas thought that a franchise should have a life span of two years, while Whitehead believed it should last in perpetuity. Also, Thomas didn't care if a franchise had no experience in the bottling business; Whitehead, on the other hand, preferred to sell Coca-Cola franchises only to experienced bottlers.

Two Girls Drink Coca-Cola
The 1912 printing of the Coca-Cola promotional calendar was the first ever to feature two models. Since 1891, Coca-Cola has issued at least one calendar every year. However, no examples are known to exist from the years 1905 and 1906. *Courtesy of The Coca-Cola Company*

Visit Our Modern Plant Car

Right: In 1929 the American Bottlers of Carbonated Beverages (A.B.C.B.) turned to several leading chemists to develop higher industry standards for sanitation in bottling factories. A Voluntary Sanitary Code, the result of the team's efforts, was published in 1929. The industry hoped that this new creed would encourage greater attention to the sanitary aspects of bottling plants and assure consumers a safe, quality product. With the development of stainless-steel equipment in 1930, new plants were much improved in the area of cleanliness. This Coca-Cola bottling plant in Cambridge, Massachusetts, even encouraged the public to tour their facilities! *Courtesy of The Coca-Cola Company*

Drink a Bottle of Carbonated Coca-Cola

Facing page: Paper products have always been an inexpensive and stylish medium of advertising display. The Coca-Cola Company produced a variety of colorful pieces in this cost-effective medium, including blotters, bookmarks, and coupons. Of these items, blotters were the most popular. Their handy size and shape were the perfect canvas for colorful illustrations, ad slogans, and informative product messages. This 1905 blotter features "The Most Refreshing Drink in the World." *Courtesy of The Coca-Cola Company*

In 1900, the two amicably agreed to go their separate ways and divide the national bottling rights between them. Whitehead delineated America into regions, and Thomas received first choice of the resulting territories. Thomas chose the East Coast, the Middle Atlantic States, and the Pacific Coast. Whitehead was left with the Southeast, Southwest, and Midwest. The result was the formation of what became known as "parent" bottlers. Thomas ran the Coca-Cola Bottling Company (often referred to as the Thomas Company) and the Whitehead/Lupton team headed the Dixie Coca-Cola Bottling Company.

In 1901, the parent companies granted franchises in Chicago, Illinois; Cincinnati, Ohio; Louisville, Kentucky; Norfolk, Virginia; and Rome, Georgia. But it was a slow start for the bottlers as only 34 new bottling plants were opened in 1902. But by 1905 automation and improved bottling equipment eased production, and 119 plants were churning out bottled Coca-Cola.

In 1909, the number of bottling plants jumped to 418! That year, more than 100 Coca-Cola bottlers met at the Aragon Hotel in Atlanta, Georgia, for first bottling convention in the soda's history. By the time the convention ended, rumors were circulating that a franchise to bottle Coca-Cola was like a license to print money. What began as a trickle turned into a torrent. Although soda fountains continued to provide Coca-Cola by the glass, it was the portable bottled Coca-Cola that came to symbolize American culture.

Secret Ingredients Made the Magic

The Enduring Mystique of Coca-Cola

Hilda Clark Calendar

Facing page: The 1903 Coca-Cola calendar featured a vivacious singer and actress of the age, Hilda Clark. The elegant Clark first posed for lithographic art in 1899. Coca-Cola and the Massengale Advertising Agency used several versions of her image until 1904. This image was copyrighted in 1902 by the Coca-Cola Company, and the calendar was published by Wolf & Company of Philadelphia, Pennsylvania. Note the branded glass holder typical of the era. *Courtesy of The Coca-Cola Company*

Lillian Nordica Calendar

Right: At 3¾ by 7 inches, the Coca-Cola calendar for 1908 was a handy size for displaying at the local soda fountain. That year, Coca-Cola debuted the slogan: "The drink that cheers but does not inebriate." That was good news for Metropolitan Opera star Lillian Nordica (1859–1914), often depicted in Coca-Cola advertising with a full glass nearby. *Courtesy of The Coca-Cola Company*

What's more American than apple pie? It can only be an ice-cold Coca-Cola!

Yet, Coke did not always evoke such a warm feeling of pride. At one time, Coca-Cola was plagued with a rather unsavory reputation. With scandalous additives such as coca and kola—and Candler's dogged determination to restrict dissemination of the concoction's key ingredients to the public—Coke's formula was ripe fodder for urban legend. To this day, the elusive formula so coveted by culinary pundits, flavorists, and competitors in the soda market remains a carefully guarded secret. And, keeping the formula a secret made and still makes good business sense, since anyone with the formula can easily copy Coca-Cola.

To protect the integrity and uniqueness of their product, Candler and Robinson referred to all of the ingredients in Coca-Cola as "merchandises." Instead of a name that might inadvertently give away the composition of the ingredient, they assigned each merchandise a specific number.

For example, the Coca-Cola formula contains a combination of seven specific merchandises. These merchandises include Merchandise Number 1 (sugar); Merchandise Number 2 (caramel); Merchandise Number 3 (caffeine); Merchandise Number 4 (phosphoric acid); Merchandise Number 5 (the coca and kola extracts); Merchandise Number 6 (glycerin); and finally, Merchandise Number 7X. And so the secret: Number 7X contains the basis of the distinct Coca-Cola flavor, a combination of flavorings and plant extracts.

In the book *Coca-Cola: An Illustrated History,* author Pat Watters writes that Candler carefully concealed the elements in Number 7X by removing all labels or any other identifying marks from their containers. Ingredients could only be identified by smell—a unique forte of Robinson's. To maintain secrecy, only Candler and Robinson blended this final mixture of ingredients. Invoices for these secret ingredients were even shunted away from the bookkeeper and kept under lock and key!

With these stringent rules in place, it didn't take long for the mystery of the Coca-Cola formula to become a part of American pop culture. And rightly so, as the Coca-Cola Company spokesmen have coyly admitted to the secrecy of Number 7X, having still not disclosed its composition. The hoopla surrounding this "mystery ingredient" has probably been the greatest marketing strategy in the history of the company.

In his revealing book *Big Secrets,* William Poundstone states: "There seems little doubt that Coca-Cola contained lime juice, circa 1909." When the author queried the Coca-Cola Company on the matter, he received no confirmation. Employee Bonita Holder replied: "While we are unable to comment specifically on the various flavors utilized in Coca-Cola, I can nonetheless confirm for you that Coca-Cola contains no lime juice, or any fruit juice." It's possible that a blend of other flavors has been substituted

"A Star Drink," 1906
Atlanta's Massengale Advertising Agency placed this full-color ad on the back cover of the *Theatre* magazine, June 1906. Sitting at her makeup table in full costume, this actress or singer enjoys "full service." During this period, both the Massengale and D'Arcy ad agencies were employed by Coca-Cola. To distinguish the two, Massengale signed its ads, and D'Arcy placed a "D" with an arrow through it in its ads. *Courtesy of Michael Dregni*

for lime juice. In fact, many artificial juice flavors are the result of combining several natural ingredients.

According to popular opinion, Merchandise Number 7X is thought to contain cinnamon (oil of cassia). Watters also lists vanilla as a prominent ingredient in the Coca-Cola product and states that Mr. Candler insisted on making the vanilla extract used in the drink himself. Candler personally selected only the best vanilla beans and aged the vanilla extract in wooden barrels for two years.

In his book, Watters also includes a partial list of ingredients written in Pemberton's own hand. Pemberton apparently wrote the list when he gave George Lowndes the formula as collateral against a loan. The list reads: "Phosphoric Attnc [sic] Acid, oil nutmeg, Fld Ex. coca Leaves, oil spice, oil Lemon, oil lime, oil nutmeg, citric acid, Elix. Orange, Caffeine, oil neroli."

From this list, experts in the flavoring industry were able to extrapolate the ingredients in Merchandise Number 7X. In 1960, Joseph Merory, president, chemist, and flavor technologist of Merory Flavors, Incorporated, of Boonton, New Jersey, published a book called *Food Flavorings, Composition, Manufacture, and Use.* The book contains a recipe for a cola flavor that for all intents and purposes appears to imitate Coca-Cola.

The recipe, Merory's MF 212, is a combination of four other recipes: MF 211 (Cola Nut Extract), MF 64 (Two-Fold Vanilla Extract), MF 209 (Cola Flavor Base), and MF 210 (Phosphoric Acid dilution). Coca leaves are not mentioned in the recipe. The most interesting ingredient in this list is the cola flavor base, MF 209. This important composite of ingredients included the oils of lemon, lime, cassia, nutmeg, neroli (an oil used in the perfume industry), and orange.

Although the top-secret ingredients of Number 7X have long been

1912 Coca-Cola Bathing Beauty
The first Coca-Cola bathing beauty made her debut in 1912. Her "haute couture" bathing costume included long black stockings and beach shoes. Images featuring the comely bather were distributed as trolley signs in an attempt to catch the eye of the commuter. *Courtesy of The Coca-Cola Company*

Trials and Tribulations

In 1898, a war that would drag on for twenty years erupted between Coca-Cola and the United States government. The trouble began on July 1 when Congress passed a stamp tax on all medicines. Based on the health claims Coca-Cola made in its advertising, the Internal Revenue Service classified Coca-Cola as a medicine, and Georgia's federal tax collector ordered the Coca-Cola Company to pay the tax.

Candler was outraged and promptly filed a lawsuit against the government. The IRS responded that Coca-Cola *was* a medicinal compound consisting of at least three drugs: kola, caffeine, and cocaine. Cocaine was potentially the most damaging ingredient, and the government aimed to prove it.

Dr. Charles Crampton (who worked for the Internal Revenue Service) analyzed a small sample of Coca-Cola syrup but was unable to prove that it contained any cocaine. Next, government lawyers pointed to the advertising methods used by the Coca-Cola Company, including the many Coca-Cola ads claiming that the drink was a cure for "headache and exhaustion," and "an ideal brain tonic." Weren't these advertising slogans obvious proof that Coca-Cola was being promoted as a medicine?

The trial quickly escalated into a heated debate between the two sides. Although Crampton failed to find any trace of cocaine in the drink, a key witnesses for Coca-Cola *did*. His name was Dr. George Payne, secretary of the Georgia State Board of Pharmacy. With access to advanced testing technology, he calculated that the Coca-Cola syrup contained one four-hundredth of a grain of cocaine per ounce. He testified to the court that the amount was "the merest trace . . . not enough to have any appreciable effect."

Interestingly enough, Asa Candler also testified that Coca-Cola contained a small trace of cocaine. Of course, Candler's testimony—along with the expert testimony of Dr. Payne—raised a red flag with the government. What if this minuscule amount of cocaine endangered the public health? After all, little children regularly drank this carbonated beverage!

The government called Dr. J. P. Baird, president of the Medical Association of Georgia, to the stand. Indeed, he testified: "Coca-Cola was a habit-forming drink." Furthermore, he stated: "Persons who take it freely seem to become more or less dependent on it." But he concluded with a surprising twist: "the cocaine couldn't be the cause of the addiction because there is too little of it."

That wasn't the last word on the subject. Dr. Crampton was called to testify again. He described how Coca-Cola was mostly a mixture of sugar and water, and although his tests hadn't revealed it, Crampton claimed that Coca-Cola *also* contained cocaine. On the stand, however, he admitted that a truly accurate test to

Ideal Brain Tonic 1897 Calendar
Ads like this one, which first appeared on a calendar in 1897, were key evidence in the government's legal battle against Coca-Cola. *Courtesy of The Coca-Cola Company*

determine the presence of cocaine didn't exist, and the only way to test for cocaine was to see how the body reacted to cooked-down Coca-Cola syrup. He implied (but did not directly state) that the residue of Coca-Cola syrup had numbed his tongue!

Much to the dismay of the Coca-Cola camp, Dr. Crampton's scrambled testimony supplied the public with the fuel it needed for a flurry of unsubstantiated rumors. As with all folklore, one point stood out above the rest: Coca-Cola contained enough cocaine to numb a man's tongue!

Fortunately, the jury was paying closer attention to the evidence. After only fifteen minutes of deliberation, the jury found in favor of Coca-Cola. The judge ordered the federal government to refund Coca-Cola the $29,502 in taxes already paid. Against all odds, the Coca-Cola Company had taken a stand against the government and won.

Coca-Cola gal, 1908

This 1908 ad, featured here on a Coca-Cola calendar, proclaims that Coca-Cola relieves fatigue! This may have been a reference to the sugar and caffeine content of the drink, which caused the company sticky legal problems. In 1909, the federal government seized a railroad shipment of Coca-Cola syrup in Chattanooga, Tennessee, and filed a lawsuit in federal court charging the company with criminal fraud. The feds had two charges against Coca-Cola: It was misbranded, since the name indicated that the product was made of coca and cola when it was not; and it was adulterated because it contained caffeine, then considered a dangerous drug. The trial began in March 1911, and within a month, the judge found in the firm's favor. *Courtesy of The Coca-Cola Company.*

cloaked in mystery, people are often just as curious about Merchandise Number 5—the coca and kola blend. It is a well-known fact that the coca portion of this blend was manufactured from the fluid extract of coca leaf. Logically, this dictates that John Styth Pemberton's early Coca-Cola formula contained cocaine, which readily accounts for the drink's uplifting effect.

From the moment Pemberton's French Wine of Coca (Coca-Cola's predecessor) hit the market, his name was forever associated with the coca leaf. The additive became an important point in advertising: When a small ad for Coca-Cola ran in the *Atlanta Journal* on May 29, 1886, it emphasized that the beverage contained "the properties of the wonderful Coca plant." At the time, many shared this positive opinion of cocaine. During this period, cocaine leaves were widely used in proprietary "medicines" of all kinds. In fact, the general public believed cocaine was a miracle drug that offered undiscovered health benefits to both the body and the mind.

It wasn't until the turn of the century that both public and medical opinions changed about cocaine. This resulted in part due to prohibition. By 1900, local prohibition laws turned many areas in the South dry. In the dry areas, liquor was difficult to obtain and bootleg alcohol was too costly for the poor. As a result, low-income citizens turned to other mood-altering substances. As an inexpensive, easy-to-obtain source of cocaine, Coca-Cola became the drink of choice. Instead of asking a fountain operator for a glass of Coca-Cola, some Southerners were heard to say, "Give me a Dope," or "Give me a Coke."

Once thought to be a miracle drug, cocaine was quickly starting to be thought of as the source of evil. Anything containing the smallest trace of coca leaves was suspect. In the South, where racial discrimination was rampant, an all-out, anti-cocaine frenzy took hold.

Typical Soda Fountain Interior
The typical soda fountain of the early 1900s was comprised of a few distinct elements. First, there was the opulent soda fountain that dispensed the bubbling waters and the sweet syrup. Next came the operator (later known as the soda jerk) who mixed the ingredients, and the sit-down counter bar where patrons were served, almost immediately. Cozy tables and chairs rounded out the parlor's décor, allowing customers to relax and recount the events of the day—an ice-cold glass of Coca-Cola in hand. Note the 1908 vintage "Good to the Last Drop" paper sign hung at the center left (14 by 22 inches). Rare signs of this type can fetch thousands of dollars in today's collector market. *Courtesy of The Coca-Cola Company*

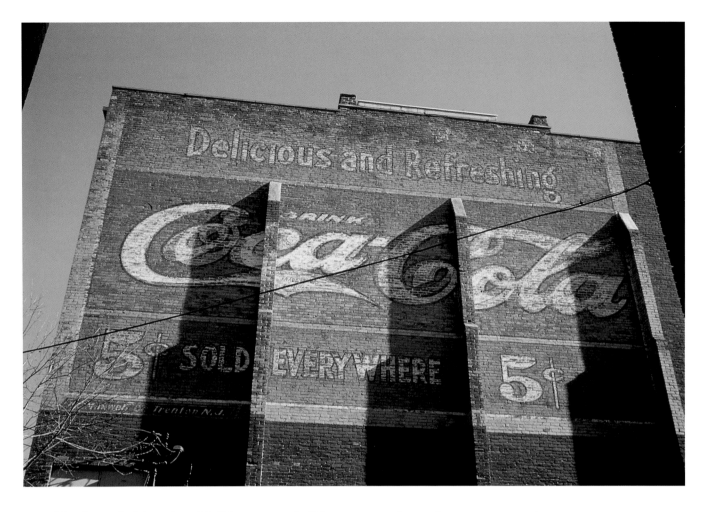

The *Journal of American Medicine* reported: "Negroes were becoming addicted to sniffing cocaine," and wild, unconfirmed stories began to spread throughout the southern United States. One particular rumor attributed superhuman powers to cocaine users, giving police departments a reason to upgrade to higher caliber weapons in order to better stop cocaine-crazed black men in their tracks.

But that wasn't all. In the *New York Tribune,* an article quoting Colonel J. W. Watson of Georgia blamed the "cocaine habit" for the many horrible crimes committed in the South by "colored people." Crazy things were happening as a result of cocaine use. In 1902, for example, a country physician in Virginia attributed a man's suicide to the excessive use of Coca-Cola. Whether this was true or not, the news scared the buying public. As a soda pop additive, cocaine was on its way out.

A crop native to Africa, the kola nut became the focus of even wilder claims. To promote kola as an ingredient, a few unabashed manufacturers took advantage of racial mythology, going so far as to say that it was the source of black men's vigor.

During this time, Johnson & Johnson began promoting a new beverage called "Kolafra," targeting the black audience for sales. A pamphlet promoting the beverage featured a picture of a muscular, bare-chested black man on the cover. The medical pundits of the age reinforced the racial hysteria when they asserted that kola was a cardiac stimulant that couldn't be tolerated by fair-skinned people.

According to Frederick Allen, author of *Secret Formula*: "It hardly mattered that Coca-Cola contained nothing but the merest trace of either drug named in its trademark. People were growing frightened. A doctor in Augusta, Georgia, said his city was filling up with 'Coca-Cola fiends' whose cravings rivaled those of opium addicts. 'Every ingredient [in Coca-Cola] is a poison,' the *Wilson Daily News*, a North Carolina publication, warned its readers, 'and not long hence, each unhappy victim of this pernicious tipple, like the opium fiend of the East, may take his neighbor by the hand, and say, "Brother, what ailed thee, to seek so dire a cure?"'"

Indeed, it appeared as if Coca-Cola was under fire from all directions. Even churches got involved. Preachers hammered home the dangers of cocaine and kola and denounced Coca-Cola as "dope." The Southern Methodist Church took an official stance against the consumption of Coca-Cola.

And, because Coca-Cola contained a trace of alcohol (from the flavoring extracts), temperance movement leaders wanted the drink abolished from American stores. The torrent of newspaper reports and editorials about the controversial drink escalated. Candler began to suspect that certain newspaper editors were not beneath a little blackmail, threatening to rake Coca-Cola over the coals since the Coca-Cola Company had refused to buy advertising space.

Some of Candler's early ads didn't help matters either, as there is no disputing their highly suggestive tone. One particular ad refers to Coca-Cola as "The Ideal Brain Tonic" that "Relieves Mental and Physical Exhaustion." This ad seems to promise more than just refreshment.

Candler now wanted nothing more than to banish all cocaine-associated rumors related to Coca-Cola, and doing so wasn't going to be easy. First, Candler had to fight back with a barrage of advertisements denouncing any trace of the drug cocaine: "Guaranteed under the Pure Food and Drug Act, June 30th, 1906, Serial #3324." Next, he glibly encouraged the use of Coca-Cola as a temperance drink: "Coca-Cola . . . the great temperance beverage—it has none of the ill effects or 'let down' qualities of alcoholic stimulants." To avoid the association between Coca-Cola and cocaine, he insisted that the public ask for his product by full name: "Nicknames encourage substitutions" and "Ask for it by its full name—then you will get the genuine."

Curiously enough, Candler continued to publish ads that featured damaging slogans. "Delicious Coca-Cola, sustains, refreshes, invigorates"; "The great temperance beverage—a liquid food for brain, body and nerves"; and "Refreshes the weary, brightens the intellect, clears the brain" were some of the more questionable standouts. Taking into account the controversy that continued to brew over the ingredients, Candler's rationale for running two contradictory campaigns remains a mystery.

Candler feared that a new law prohibiting the sale of Coca-Cola would soon to be enacted. Already worn down by the numerous legal battles over Coca-Cola trademark infringements, he gave serious consideration to sell-

DRINK Coca-Cola

At Soda Fountains
and in Bottles

Demand the genuine
by full name –

Nicknames encourage
substitution

THE COCA-COLA COMPANY
Atlanta, Ga.

ing off the brand and the secret formula. Nevertheless, Candler decided to hold off on the sale.

Today the secret formula resides inside a special security vault at the Trust Company of Georgia. The safe deposit box is marked with a red flag, and no one may view the document without the board's permission. Protocol dictates that the chairperson, president, or corporate secretary must be present when the formula is removed from the vault, and only two company officials may know the formula at any given time (their identites must not be disclosed to anyone). These two officials may never travel on the same airplane.

Exactly what are the ingredients in Coca-Cola? We may get close to deciphering the formula, but the fact is that we may never know for sure. After all, there are some things in life—Coca-Cola included, perhaps—that just are not meant to be revealed or explained. It's precisely this buzz of secrecy that continues to propel the myth of the soft drink that John Styth Pemberton brewed up so many decades ago. If you lose the secrecy, all that you have left is a simple, or perhaps complex, combination of soda water and flavorings.

At Fountains and in Bottles
Nicknames encourage substitution! When Coca-Cola initially established its brand identity, protecting the trademark was important. To keep customer confusion to a minimum and to discourage competitors from producing copycat products, Coca-Cola worked hard to protect and defend its product name, often taking creators of imitations to court. *Courtesy of The Coca-Cola Company*

Thirst Content
Every day—many times a day, it just seems as if nothing would satisfy.
Drink
Coca-Cola
TRADE MARK REGISTERED
There's nothing like it.
It's as wholesome as pure water, and quenches the thirst as nothing else will.
Delicious—Refreshing Wholesome
Demand the Genuine as made by
THE COCA-COLA CO.
ATLANTA, GA.
Our new booklet, telling of Coca Cola vindication at Chattanooga, for the asking
Whenever you see an Arrow think of Coca-Cola.

Chapter 6

A Formula For Success

Advertising and the Great American Soft Drink

Thirst Content Ad, 1912

Facing page: "When you see an arrow, think of Coca-Cola." This 1912 two-color ad appeared in national magazines of the day, such as the *Saturday Evening Post* and the *Ladies Home Journal*. Most of the early Coca-Cola color ads were produced by the Massengale and D'Arcy advertising agencies. Collectors can easily distinguish between the two: Massengale signed its ads, and D'Arcy placed a little "D" with an arrow through it in its ads. Check the lower left-hand corner of this ad, just above the text within the border. *Coolstock.com Advertising Archives*

Coca-Cola Lillian Nordica Premium

Right: Lillian Nordica, the sweetheart of the American opera received her vocal training in Boston, Massachusetts, at the New England Conservatory and went on to study in Milan, Italy, where she made her operatic debut in 1879. In 1883, the stunning brunette debuted in America at the New York Academy of Music. She first sang at the Metropolitan Opera on December 18, 1891, and remained with the company for eleven seasons. While on tour in 1914, the *Tasman,* a ship she was traveling on, slammed into a coral reef off the coast of Indonesia, where it remained for three days. Nordica suffered from exposure and died on May 10, 1914, on the island of Java. This rare 1905 "Lillian Nordica" promotion piece is a celluloid hanging sign framed in metal. *Courtesy of The Coca-Cola Company*

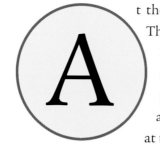

1912 Hamilton King

Hamilton King, born in Lewiston, Maine, studied at the Academie Julian in Paris and became an illustrator, painter, and etcher. A member of the Society of Illustrators, he was a resident primarily of East Hampton, New York, where he died in 1952. During his heyday, he painted many memorable advertising pieces for the Coca-Cola Company, including this 1912 calendar. *Courtesy of The Coca-Cola Company*

A t the turn of the century, marketing was in its infancy. There were no focus groups, surveys, or market research. In fact, the concept of consumerism hadn't yet fully taken shape. Folks simply didn't feel the need to buy products. Until the turn of the century, anything that a family required had been crafted at home or purchased at the local general store.

Such a way of getting goods caused a problem: With the Industrial Revolution underway, factories were cranking out a surplus of products—with few buyers. It was necessary, indeed urgent, that demand for these goods be created. The field of advertising emerged, and the purpose of this new industry was to create and sustain consumer demand.

The advertising agency as we know it today was still a relatively new phenomena in America at the turn of the century. Advertising existed as an extension of the old advertising brokerage system that had been established in the late 1890s. These agencies purchased large blocks of print space from newspapers and magazines at discounted prices and then resold the space to merchants and companies who wished to advertise their products and services. As a sideline, they also provided illustrations, and sometimes, highly informative copy. But these creative services were basic at best. Their sole focus was on selling space in the press media.

The Massengale Advertising Agency—one of the Coca-Cola Company's most visible and successful promoters—evolved from this type of agency. Its first ads for the Coca-Cola beverage reflected the simple practices of the brokerage system. There was no attempt to convey Coke as a dynamic product. Highly stylized, Massengale's illustrations focused on the Coca-Cola drinking people and their settings while copy enticed readers with details of Coca-Cola's characteristics and benefits.

Massengale wasn't afraid to experiment, however. Early Massengale ads suggest that the agency was not opposed to trying psychological marketing techniques. In such ads, illustrations depicted men and women in pleasant surroundings, doing pleasant things. The idea was that prospective buyers would relate to the people in the images and imagine themselves drinking Coca-Cola, too. These ads were the first created to relate a particular food product, such as a soft drink, to a specific attitude and feeling.

With only a handful of advertising mediums available at the time, drumming up desire for a product proved to be a challenge. Newspapers and magazines topped the list as advertising outlets, followed by streetcar billboards, pamphlets, and handbills. With the advent of four-color printing, once-colorless magazines took on a fresh appearance. Because of their appealing look, national magazines gained a newfound, loyal following among women. Glamour became the focal point of many publications, while the home—and products related to the home followed closely behind.

DRINK
Coca-Cola
DELICIOUS
AND
REFRESHING

1914 Betty Calendar
"Betty," the model for the 1914 Coca-Cola calendar, was featured on many of the brand's advertising items that year, including change trays, serving trays, signs, posters, and more. Because of this, Betty is fondly remembered by more people than any of the other Coca-Cola models. "Exhilarating, Refreshing" was the new slogan for 1914. *Courtesy of The Coca-Cola Company*

Coca-Cola Remembered

Recent marketing studies have revealed a link between specific colors and desired consumer reactions. Whether on a package, advertisement, or building, color influences the thoughts of a potential buyer. In the beginning, the Coca-Cola Company did not have marketing studies or focus groups, but its founders certainly knew the importance of color. It is not by chance that red, green, and white were chosen to exemplify the Coca-Cola brand. Red, the primary color for Coca-Cola (developed by Asa Candler), symbolizes energy. Green evokes coolness, the sensation of sinking a bare foot into a grass lawn on a hot summer day. White embodies purity. Together the colors became an emblem for Coca-Cola, much like a flag is for a nation. ©2001 Pedar Ness, Coolstock.com

This phenomenon was duly noted by Asa Candler, who promptly dedicated $10,000 in advertising for the placement of magazine ads in *Munsey's Monthly*. Candler hired the Massengale Advertising Agency of Atlanta, Georgia, to dream up a concept, create the illustrations, and write the copy for the first Coca-Cola advertisements to appear in a national publication.

In a 1902 edition of *Munsey's Monthly*, vivid color illustrations by Henry Hutt showed men and women enjoying glasses of Coca-Cola in lush surroundings.

No doubt the response expected from consumers was a positive one: In short order, the Coca-Cola Company's magazine ad campaign was expanded to include other publications. As other beverages battled for notoriety, would-be soft-drink purchasers were assailed with the virtues of Coca-Cola in the *Housewife*, the *Housekeeper*, *American Theater*, *Saturday Evening Post*, and the *Literary Digest*.

Unfortunately, placing ads was sometimes a hit or miss proposition. A company could not scientifically measure the success of advertising dollars spent. Instead, an ad campaign's success was measured in the amount of revenue it appeared to generate. And Coca-Cola syrup sales were rising. As a result, the annual marketing budget's increase was in direct proportion to sales. By 1903, the Coca-Cola Company was spending $200,000 on all facets of sales promotion. Advertising had become a way of life for the Coca-Cola Company.

Around this same time, Samuel Dobbs was in the Midwest meeting with William Cheever D'Arcy, a salesman from an agency in St. Louis who was selling advertising space on streetcars. D'Arcy and Dobbs hit it off famously, becoming fast friends. As it would later turn out, this friendship would mark a turning point in the Coca-Cola Company's marketing strategy.

In 1906, D'Arcy was busy building his business. He secured an arrangement with Cascade Whiskey, his first client, and promptly opened his own advertising agency in St. Louis. As it happened, Asa Candler made Samuel Dobbs the director of the Coca-Cola Company's advertising that same year. In turn, Dobbs turned to his new friend to provide the print ads for the St. Louis and Kansas City, Missouri, area. With a total budget of $4,602, it was a small start for D'Arcy, but it was one that held much promise. The following year, D'Arcy secured a $25,000 account with Coca-Cola.

Dobbs's money was put to good use. D'Arcy had a certain flair for recognizing gifted illustrators, and he quickly secured the talents of many unknown artists. A few of his first choices, including Norman Rockwell

Victorian Girl Coca-Cola Tray
Artist Hamilton King provided the image for the 10½-by-13¼-inch Coca-Cola serving tray in 1909, an image known as "The Coca-Cola Girl." It was manufactured in Conshoctin, Ohio, by American Art Works, Incorporated. Well over one million reproductions of this tray were turned out in the early seventies. *Courtesy of The Coca-Cola Company*

and W. C. Wyeth, became famous artists in their own right. Armed with a troop of talented freelancers and in-house illustrators, D'Arcy set about creating desire for Coca-Cola by linking it to emotion. This marked the first time in the history of Coca-Cola that an advertisement aimed to evoke a particular feeling.

Like Massengale, D'Arcy employed slice-of-life scenes. But D'Arcy had the ability to reach into the common man's heart, bringing the advertisement to life. D'Arcy replaced the starched, stiff, pretty girl of previous years with a more relaxed, accessible person, to whom the common consumer could easily relate. While the featured girl maintained a wholesome appearance, D'Arcy made her more flirtatious, creating a link between Coca-Cola and romance.

While D'Arcy relied on outside artists to do the artwork, he always wrote the advertising copy himself. A natural salesman, D'Arcy's words conjured up just the right amount of sizzle to pull readers into the ad to make them want to buy. He was a firm believer that "advertising is selling," and that the more people you can reach with your message, the more you can sell. For this reason, newspapers—with their wide coverage and large readership—were his favorite advertising medium.

Men comprised a large part of the nation's newspaper readership. Right after he acquired the Coca-Cola account, D'Arcy altered his marketing strategy to reach this audience. In 1906, he hired Ty Cobb, a prominent baseball player and much-loved sports hero of the time, to appear in an ad. D'Arcy's "athletes praise Coca-Cola" strategy included other well-known baseball players from the Chicago White Sox and Cubs, St. Louis Cardinals, Philadelphia A's, and St. Louis Browns.

The sport of baseball and its pantheon of heroes had a magnetic appeal to both men and boys. D'Arcy used America's favorite pastime to create a link between this popular game and Coca-Cola. It was as easy as rounding the bases on a home run. The success of this sports-related campaign made D'Arcy realize the power in marketing Coca-Cola to different groups. To be most successful, he had to create Coca-Cola ads that appealed to *all* Americans—men, women, and children alike.

With the success of the sports campaign under his belt, D'Arcy turned the direction of Coca-Cola advertising to his first love: billboards. But D'Arcy, who had a real knack for showmanship, wasn't satisfied with the static billboards that perched on the tops of buildings or that bordered the roadways.

1913 Coca-Cola Tray
One of today's most-popular Coke collectibles, metal trays advertising the Coca-Cola brand were made from tin plate. Round, oval, and rectangular serving trays and change trays were the most common examples of this promotional item. Until 1926, female models (like the girl shown here) were used exclusively. Artist Hamilton King's signature appears on this 1913 tray. *Courtesy of The Coca-Cola Company*

Instead, he and Samuel Dobbs designed what was to become the world's largest animated sign. In 1908, the eye-catching wonder was strategically placed on the main railway line between Philadelphia and New York. The thirty-two-foot-high curiosity portrayed a soda jerk drawing a glass of Coca-Cola from a ceramic dispenser. Water colored to look like Coca-Cola flowed directly into the glass from a two-inch pipe connected to a water main! Commuters were treated to an eye-catching feast of flowing Coca-Cola.

With outdoor theater like this, it wasn't long before Coca-Cola and its advertising efforts caught the attention of the advertising industry. In 1909, the Associated Advertising Clubs of America named Coca-Cola "the best advertised article in America." Of course, an advertising budget of more than $760,000 may have contributed to the sudden ubiquity of Coke. By 1910, D'Arcy was spending a whopping $225,000 of the Coca-Cola Company's marketing dollars. By 1913, D'Arcy had full control of the Coca-Cola advertising account, a relationship that would last for more than fifty years.

Two Bottles Coca-Cola Sign
This circa 1930s Coca-Cola sign featuring two embossed hobble-skirt bottles echoes a design produced in 1908 that featured two straight-side bottles with paper labels. *Courtesy of The Coca-Cola Company*

Chapter 7

Towards Sweeter Times

Coca-Cola and the Sugar Crisis

1916 World War I Girl

Facing page: In 1916, Coca-Cola issued what would be later known by collectors as the "World War I Girl." This rose-loving beauty appeared one year later on change and serving trays. *Courtesy of The Coca-Cola Company*

Don't Waste Sugar Cartoon

Right: During World War I, a sugar shortage prompted the government to request that the public tone down its sugar consumption. This cartoon featuring two patrons at the local soda fountain explained why, in hopes of curbing the public's collective sweet tooth. Sugar meant ships. The ocean-going transports that were once used to carry the sweet substance were now needed to ferry troops. *National Archives via Coolstock.com*

Sugar means **Ships**

The sugar used in sweet drinks must be brought to America in ships. Last year 400,000,000 lbs of sugar were imported for sweet drinks. These ships must now be used to carry soldiers to the front

Drink less sweetened beverages

We are at war

Every Spoonful — Every Sip — Means less for a Fighter

U. S. Food Administration.

ICE CREAM AND ICE COLD SODA

1920 Coca-Cola Serving Tray
Up until 1920, Coca-Cola trays were typically made in one size. Sometimes trays were available in two different sizes and every so often in three sizes. Trays remain one of the top Coca-Cola collectibles to this day, the rarest examples easily fetching thousands of dollars. *Courtesy of The Coca-Cola Company*

By 1914, the Coca-Cola Company was nearing a pinnacle in terms of national brand-name recognition and consumer confidence. For most Americans who drank carbonated beverages, it was the cola drink of choice. Be it at the soda fountain or from a bottle, Coca-Cola sales were high, and business was good.

The past few years, however, had been stressful for Asa Candler. Multiple lawsuits over trademark infringement, problems with the government's Pure Food and Drug Act, and increasing competitiveness within the company had all taken a toll on Candler, who slowly began to extricate himself from the day-to-day activities of the Coca-Cola Company, and transferred the responsibilities of acting president to his son, Charles Howard Candler.

In 1916, the year he turned sixty-three, Asa Candler was elected to a two-year term as the mayor of Atlanta, Georgia. Candler made his final break from the Coca-Cola Company on Christmas Day that same year, dividing his shares of Coca-Cola stock between his wife and his five children and keeping seven shares for himself.

Howard Candler, the acting de facto president, attempted to keep the company on solid financial ground and quell any negative repercussions of Asa's departure. Although Asa Candler hadn't been actively involved in the daily affairs of the Coca-Cola Company since 1913, he was nevertheless the symbolic mainstay of the firm. With his absence now official, the Coca-Cola Company was forced to reorganize and restructure. Unfortunately, neither Asa nor any of his contemporaries could have predicted what was about to happen next.

On April 6, 1917, the United States Congress declared war on Germany. For the first time in the history of the nation, America was called upon to provide its food to hungry civilians in other nations. Plus, America needed to feed its troops during the war. Although America had always enjoyed a surplus of comestibles before the war, extraordinary demand strained available supplies.

To tackle this problem, Herbert Hoover, the United States Food Administration (USFA) Secretary at the time, formed the all-volunteer Food Conservation Army. The Food Conservation Army taught Americans how to conserve and stretch their food supplies: "From our fields and orchards and gardens we must feed and clothe our hundred million of men, women and children, supply our armies, and feed a large part of the population of Europe, where the need is far greater than here." The USFA insured that there were adequate and reasonably priced food supplies for civilians and military alike.

1919 Miss Marion Davies

Above: Miss Marion Davies was an actress and film star. In 1919, the year this calendar debuted, Coca-Cola issued two calendars: one featuring a celebrity and the other an anonymous model. *Courtesy of The Coca-Cola Company*

1918 Beach Girls

Above, right: A day at the beach was the motif for this 1918 Coca-Cola calendar. By this time, Coca-Cola could be purchased at the nearby beach pavilion in glasses and in bottles. Ads such as this are powerful windows to the style and fashions of the day. Although it looks as if the seated girl is wearing a light summer outfit, she is in fact wearing the typical bathing suit of the era. *Courtesy of The Coca-Cola Company*

During this time, feelings of patriotism ran high. American manufacturers were eager to help the war effort. Corporate advertising took on a new attitude, evoking the theme of patriotism and calling for consumers to conserve. Of course, the Coca-Cola Company fell right into step with this newfound nationalism. The headline in a 1917 magazine advertisement for Coca-Cola read: "Making a Soldier of Sugar." In this particular ad, the company promised to abide by the government's regulations in the effort to conserve supplies, such as sugar. It was an oath that was soon to be tested.

In October 1917, Herbert Hoover announced that all syrup manufacturers would be limited to a half quota of their previous year's consumption! This was big news for Coca-Cola and other companies whose products depended on a steady supply of sugar. This rationing severely curtailed Coca-Cola syrup production. Coca-Cola experimented with other sweeteners such as corn syrup, glucose, and beet sugar—all the while promising consumers that they would not compromise product quality.

But nothing could wean the public from their addiction to pure cane sugar. Without sugar, the sales of soft drinks plummeted. For the duration of the war, the Coca-Cola Company (and many others like it) resigned itself to zero profitability. The pursuit of profits and growth were put on hold in favor of survival.

When World War I ended on November 11, 1918, Americans celebrated by dancing in the streets. American soft drink makers couldn't muster such enthusiasm. Even after the war was over, sugar rationing continued, forcing many soft drink companies to go out of business. Others, including Coca-Cola, were still reeling from the enormous monetary losses they had suffered.

But the Coca-Cola Company wasn't discouraged. D'Arcy designed a print advertisement that succinctly broadcast the company's stand on the sugar crisis. The headline shouted: "Victory's Reward means Volume Restored." The copy did its part to reassure the public that things would return to the way they had been: "Pending readjustment of the world's sugar supply, our output of Coca-Cola will remain limited until the need of conservation shall no longer exist. Meanwhile Coca-Cola will live up to its past, and we in common with other American business, look hopefully to restoration of the happy normal."

By 1919, the government lifted all sugar rationing restrictions. Now Coca-Cola really had something to celebrate. Soon thereafter, the pent-up demand for Coca-Cola resulted in a syrup sales bonanza. Nineteen billion gallons of syrup flowed into bottles or glasses! According to Frederick Allen, author of *Secret Formula,* this equated to "an average of thirty Cokes a year for every man, woman, and child in the United States." Indeed, "Victory's Reward was Volume Restored," and the Coca-Cola Company went on to exceed the "happy normal" of D'Arcy's ad.

1922 Baseball Scene
In 1922, Coca-Cola continued its calendar line with another image of an anonymous model. This time, she enjoys a baseball game while indulging in a glass of Coca-Cola. Instead of relying on the fountain to mix her drink, she uses a handy glass bottle containing the premixed beverage. The question is: What did she do with the glass when she was done? *Courtesy of The Coca-Cola Company*

Coca-Cola sales improved for other reasons, too. After decades of fighting for the eradication of alcohol, the Woman's Christian Temperance Union (W.C.T.U.) achieved victory in 1919. The government passed the Eighteenth Amendment to the Constitution, prohibiting the manufacture and distribution of all alcoholic beverages. Ironically, the very same government that had plagued the Coca-Cola Company for decades with an ongoing lawsuit now became the unwitting instrument of its growth. Without their beer, wine, and other distilled spirits, people turned to soft drinks like Coca-Cola.

The resulting increase in sales made Coca-Cola the largest consumer of cane sugar in the world. Unfortunately, this made Coca-Cola quite vulnerable, since the nation's sugar problems were far from over. As it happened, the war shortages created an artificial demand for sugar, causing the government to cap the price at nine cents per pound. The real problems began on December 1, 1919, when the price restriction was lifted. Commodities speculators drove the price of sugar into the stratosphere, and in just a few short weeks, prices soared from nine cents a pound to twenty cents per pound.

Prohibition Raid 1920s

A police raid conducted by law officers in Dallas, Texas, during the Prohibition days of the Roaring Twenties uncovered a lot of illegal liquor. While the many patrons of underground bars known as speakeasies guzzled down alcohol, the rest of America was trying to get by without distilled spirits. Indulging in soda pop and ice cream concoctions became popular alternatives during this time. *Texas/Dallas History and Archives Division, Dallas Public Library*

Superior Drug Serves Coke
Even after Prohibition faded into memory, the drugstore soda fountain remained one of the most popular spots to obtain an ice-cold Coca-Cola (and other treats). All across America, the drugstore endured as a mainstay of Main Street and small-town commerce. Like today's mall, it's where people came to meet, relax, and enjoy the simple things that made life worth living. *Courtesy of The Coca-Cola Company*

With this increase, the Coca-Cola Company was caught between the proverbial rock and a hard place: On the one hand, the demand for Cola syrup was at an all time high, which meant the company should be making a profit; on the other hand, the syrup manufacturing cost was prohibitively expensive. Cutting back on syrup production was not an option. The only solution was to corner as much of the sugar supply as possible.

It was during this crisis that the Coca-Cola Company became a publicly held corporation. On September 12, 1919, a group of investment banks lead by Ernest Woodruff purchased the Coca-Cola Company from the Candler family and other private stockholders for a grand total of $25 million—$15 million in cash and $10 million in preferred stock. Samuel Dobbs was named as the new president, and Charles Howard Candler was named as the chairman of the board. Later that same month, Coca-Cola common stock went public and appeared on the New York Stock Exchange under the symbol "KO." The American public—not aware that the company was in severe financial difficulty—went into an all-out buying frenzy.

Despite the enthusiasm of the new investors, the now-public corporation was immediately besieged by the affects of the sugar crisis. During the spring of 1920, sugar prices shot up to an all-time high of twenty-eight cents per pound. In response to this price hike, Howard Candler contacted a number of large sugar refineries and importers and negotiated the purchase of a six-month supply at twenty-eight cents per pound. But shortly after making this deal, sugar prices stopped rising, hovered at twenty-eight cents per pound for a short time, and, in August, plummeted to ten cents per pound. The fall in price was very bad news for the Coca-Cola Company, which was now stuck with a commitment to purchase $8 million of sugar at twenty-eight cents per pound!

In response, Dobbs launched a vigorous advertising campaign that autumn, in an attempt to sell more Coca-Cola more quickly. Normally, advertising for soft drinks slowed at the close of the summer syrup season, but Dobbs proposed something unique: Why not position Coca-Cola as a "year-round" beverage? So began the soon-to-be-famous "Thirst Knows No Season" campaign. Coca-Cola allocated $100,000 a month to newspaper advertising alone!

The timing was right for such an optimistic campaign. Many Americans reveled in the post-war boom of the 1920s. Women had won the right to vote, mass production was in full swing, and American youth were discarding the prim Victorian ways of their parents. A nonstop party ensued, kicking off what many referred to as the Jazz Age. A nation on a serious spending spree eagerly bought up luxury goods, homes, automobiles, furs, clothing, and jewelry.

Of course, Coca-Cola came along for the ride. People were once again indulging in the bubbly beverage. It wasn't long before the stockpiles of overpriced sugar had disappeared. The company's debt dropped and revenues increased. Against all odds, Coca-Cola had weathered the ups and downs of the sugar crisis and emerged intact.

1925 Girl at Party
An elegant girl attending a classy social gathering graced the Coca-Cola calendar in 1925. As it happened, "Enjoy the sociable drink" was the new slogan of the year, a perfect accompaniment to the high-society motif of the calendar. *Courtesy of The Coca-Cola Company*

Chapter 8

Coca-Cola Comes of Age, 1919–1928

Advertising During the Golden Years

Coke Cooler at the Gas Pumps

Facing page: In 1928, the first chest-style Coca-Cola coolers were a big hit with retail proprietors. At general stores and filling stations across the land, basic models produced by the Glasscock Brothers Manufacturing Company served the modern motorist. Unlike today's refrigerated dispensing machines, these simple bottle bins used cracked ice (made from large blocks), most likely delivered by another vestige of a forgotten era: the iceman. *Courtesy of The Coca-Cola Company*

Streamline Coca-Cola Truck

Right: The Coca-Cola Company Standardization Committee adopted uniform colors for their trucks in 1925. In 1929, *Coca-Cola Bottlers' Standards* specified that trucks should be yellow and red, with black hoods, fenders, and radiators. During the 1930s and 1940s, the Weldmech Steel Products Company of Hattiesburg, Mississippi, made "full streamline" trailer bodies for commercial soda pop bottle delivery trucks. This handsome unit boasted a built-in sign box for carrying road signs, a rear bumper, torpedo-type running boards with one-piece pressed steel drop panels, crown fenders, and lights in the rear panels. Plenty of room was allotted for display of the brand name, both at the top of the trailer and at the rear. *Preziosi, Coolstock.com*

It was during these years of wild abandon that former reporter Archie Lee joined the D'Arcy Advertising Agency. With his innate knack for advertising, Archie created one of the most imaginative campaigns in the history of Coca-Cola. The 1922 four-color magazine ad featured a beautiful young woman gliding on a pair of skis, with a backdrop of snowy hills. Snowflakes adorned her smiling face and the slogan proclaimed: "Thirst Knows No Season." The message was clear: Coke was a drink to be enjoyed anywhere—anytime.

Lee later collaborated with Robert Winship Woodruff (elected Coca-Cola president on April 28, 1923), and together they ushered in the golden age of Coke advertising. The pair spent hours brainstorming. They wanted the public to view Coke as a facet of American life, an icon as American as the Fourth of July. In his book *Secret Formula,* Frederick Allen quotes Woodruff as saying: "We wanted to promote Coca-Cola not just as a soft drink or even as 'the leading' soft drink. We wanted to promote it as something bigger than just the answer to thirst."

Indeed, Lee was a shrewd advertising man. Deep down, he knew that the key to the public's heart was to portray Coca-Cola as more than just a product—Coke had to represent something intangible, such as a joyful lifestyle. And so, a total revamp of the Coca-Cola marketing campaign was in order. Realizing that Coca-Cola lacked product identity, Lee went to work on Coca-Cola's logo and trademark. He maintained the curly script as Frank Robinson had designed it, but he placed the words "Coca-Cola" within a rectangle. Later, he created the round, red sign with the white Coca-Cola logo. Lee's plan worked, and Coca-Cola soon became the world's most-recognized trademark.

The logo and trademark were just the beginning, however. Lee hired talented artists who excelled at creating emotion and movement on canvas. The first artist to design new ads and calendars for Coke was Haddon Sundblom, also credited with the creation of Aunt Jemima and the Quaker Oats man. Sundblom's first step in learning the company philosophy was to acquaint himself with the holy trinity of colors used in Coca-Cola ads: red, white, and green. He learned that the red, white and green combination was much more than a temporary device of harmonious color. These colors were planned: RED stood for energy, WHITE for pure wholesomeness, GREEN for refreshing coolness.

Sundblom proved to be a quick learner. In 1924, he completed his first canvas for Coca-Cola—the image of a lovely young woman wearing an ivory-colored dress, sitting at a soda fountain and facing the public. The woman was the epitome of femininity, with a hint of flirtation. Lee also ventured into other directions to reinforce his dynamic ad strategy.

Refresh Yourself Ad, 1924
The time on the young lady's wristwatch read 12:20, no doubt the perfect time for her lunchtime glass of Coca-Cola. What's interesting to note in this ad is that the woman is alone, enjoying herself, unbothered. Who needs a man around when you have a refreshing soft drink to keep you company? Published in the September 1924 issue of the *Pictorial Review.* Coolstock.com Advertising Archives

The Ritz Boy
This 1925 ad was a recreation of Coca-Cola's first billboard, a graphic that featured a hotel bellhop nicknamed the Ritz Boy (possibly a takeoff on the opulence of the famous Ritz Hotel). The first billboard went up in May 1925, with more to follow. In the five-month ad campaign, the accommodating Ritz Boy (depicted with four other subjects) appeared on billboards in 5,270 cities across America. The ad blitz was a major investment, sponsored by the Coca-Cola Company and 893 bottlers.
Courtesy of The Coca-Cola Company

Drink Coke in Bottles Sign

This diminutive 23-by-6-inch embossed tin sign was produced circa 1922. During the 1920s, roadside businesses posted such "snipe" signs, featuring products of all kinds, from chewing tobacco to sewing needles. Businesses of the day promoted a hodgepodge of products. The conglomeration of signs and competing images probably confused the consumer more than anything else. *Courtesy of The Coca-Cola Company*

The image portrayed in the 1925 "Ritz Boy" billboard was an early example of Lee's advertising savvy. Featuring a bellboy dressed in a crisp, white uniform that resembled one of the eager bellhops employed at the famous Ritz hotels, the billboard conjured up a world of leisure. Holding a tray with a bottle of Coke along with the familiar bell-shaped Coca-Cola glass, the lad seemed to step right out of the billboard, ready to serve *you*. The oversized sign was a winner, and Coca-Cola had more than five thousand of them installed along the roadsides of every major American town and city.

Lee also embedded themes of first love into the Coca-Cola ad campaign. He employed the usual "boy meets girl" theme used in the films and romance novels of the age, but he took the theme a step further. According to Frederick Allen: "For the first time, ads not only showed boy-meeting-girl, but suggested pointedly that boy and girl somehow were meeting *because* of Coca-Cola." Such an idea was a leap into new territory for product advertisements.

During this time, the media had become the best source of information on social change. The nation's magazines, radio stations, and newspapers delivered words and images of the latest fads, including a "flapper," an indomitable young woman who modeled herself after the French prostitute of World War I. A flapper tended to be an outspoken girl with short, bobbed hair, a flat chest, rolled-up stockings, and a hiked-up hemline; she smoked, cussed, and indulged. A far cry from the Victorian "pretty girl" of Candler's era, Coca-Cola featured a slightly subdued "Flapper Girl" image on their 1923 advertising calendar.

Such subdued imagery was short-lived. In 1924, Coca-Cola unveiled an even bolder calendar model. Sporting a come-hither smile, she was clad in an even more revealing outfit than her predecessor. Coke's famed "pretty girls" had shed their modesty to emerge as seductive sirens, each one more scantily clad than the last.

Such was Lee's style. He utilized every media venue, designing brighter and bolder lithographs, billboards, and magazine ads—ads that portrayed activities with which the public could personally identify. Lee's ads expressed how a bottle of Coke would satisfy all needs, including the desire for wealth. To convey these messages, Lee replaced lengthy copy with short, catchy slogans. Each slogan proclaimed that Coke was not just a product, it was the path to enjoyment, fulfillment, and success—a path to a better life!

1923 Flapper Girl

The "Flapper Girl" appearing in this 1923 calendar held a glass of Coca-Cola. A second version of the calendar featured the exact same image, except she held a bottle instead of the glass. That year, "Enjoy Thirst" emerged as the latest advertising slogan. *Courtesy of The Coca-Cola Company*

Lee broke ground with the first of these modern advertisements in 1923. The first ad to appear in magazines was a colorful, action-packed image of a young woman, rope in hand, taming a water-skiing board. The slogan simply read: "Drink Coca-Cola Delicious and Refreshing." The woman's smiling face implied that she really enjoyed a bottle of Coke (that is, before she ventured off into choppier waters). The hidden meaning: Coca-Cola provides energy, enhances the enjoyment of life, and puts people on the cutting edge.

Lee followed these new ads with a series of memorable slogans. Catchy phrases such as: "Enjoy Thirst"; "When you get a good thirst—treat it right"; "Refresh yourself"; "There's nothing like it when you're thirsty"; "Always delightful"; "Enjoy thirst through all four seasons"; "A perfect blend of pure product from nature"; and "You'll enjoy it too" gradually altered the public's attitude towards Coca-Cola. The beverage once consumed to relieve a headache was now sipped just for the fun of it.

By the mid 1920s, Americans enjoyed prosperity like never before. As their wages rose, their work weeks dropped from sixty to forty-eight hours. Skilled labor was in short supply, with unemployment at an all time low of 1.3 percent. The American workforce was bursting at the seams. Archie Lee took notice and began to target the workingman and -woman. In 1924, he introduced the slogan "Pause and Refresh Yourself," a phrase encouraging workers to reach for an ice-cold Coca-Cola instead of a hot cup of coffee.

By 1925, Lee's strategic ad campaign was well underway. As consumers fell in love with the indulgences of the age, the new advertising angle was to get inside their head, push the right buttons, and inspire them to buy. To make this happen, ad men like Lee played off consumers' insecurities, delusions, and attachments.

Just attracting consumers to Coca-Cola was no longer sufficient. Ads had to motivate people to actually go out and buy the product. Accompanied with just the right imagery, slogans like: "Thirst is discriminating"; "It Had to Be Good to Get Where It Is"; "Everybody likes it"; "Refreshment Time"; "Continuous Quality"; and "The sociability of thirst" led thirsty customers to the cash register like never before.

Print ads weren't the only medium. By 1927, more than six million households owned a radio. In fact, the radio console became the center of family entertainment. At first, advertisers weren't aware of radio's potential as a commercial medium. But after networks such as the National Broadcasting Corporation went nationwide, advertisers jumped at the opportunity to explore this new medium's commercial potential.

Lee seized this new opportunity to break new ground. Unlike the majority of other advertisers, Coca-Cola would do more than just sponsor a radio broadcast; instead, Coke would *be* the broadcast! Lee and Woodruff worked together to create a dynamic story that became the forerunner of the modern soap opera, a romance story that embodied all

Coca-Cola Handy Six Pack Container
Above: In 1922, Harrison Jones envisioned the six-bottle carton as a way to get Coca-Cola into more homes. At the time, transporting Coca-Cola by the caseload was cumbersome. There was little doubt that a smaller pack of six, sold for only twenty-five cents, would be a hit. The six-pack carton, introduced in 1924, was slow to catch on at first. But by 1939, seventy million Americans picked up the so-called "handle of invitation" and carried the cartons home. *Courtesy of The Coca-Cola Company*

1924 Smiling Girl
Facing page: The "Smiling Girl" appeared on the Coca-Cola calendar of 1924. "Always a Delightful Surprise" was the Coca-Cola slogan currently in vogue. Perhaps that's the reason for the smile? *Courtesy of The Coca-Cola Company*

No Drip Bottle Protector
Above: The no drip bottle protector was a clever advertising accessory patented on June 14, 1927. How did this wax-paper drinking aid work? The idea was to slip your soda pop bottle into the no drip protector sack, thereby ensuring that you would catch all of the condensation and dripping water. Without it, the icy-cold droplets fell right into your lap or onto the front seat of your brand new convertible. *Coolstock.com Collection*

Cool and Cheerful Ad 1925
Facing page: In contrast to the elegant ladies found in the era's pretty girl calendars, Coca-Cola issued periodical advertisements exhibiting a slightly different tack. Here, the young lady appears to be more like the rest of us, or as the ad states, "a wonderful girl in a real American pose—at the soda fountain." This ad appeared in the June 1925 issue of the *Ladies' Home Journal. Coolstock.com Advertising* Archives

the joy and heartache of first love. The *Coca-Cola Girl* show ran fourteen weeks on NBC and its affiliates. The show featured Vivian, the Coca-Cola girl and the object of Jim's affection. Every week, the audience tuned in to learn how their romance was developing. To hook listeners, every broadcast was a cliff-hanger, leaving the audience to speculate if Jim was worthy of Vivian or if she would dump him in favor of another. Was marriage in the cards? Would they live happily ever after? Listeners nationwide were mesmerized.

At the same time, the growth of the film industry gave rise to a new consumer attitude. Hollywood—with its plethora of new film stars—became the vanguard of everything that was hip, or square. The cleverly marketed association of actors with products created, in many Americans, an "I have to have it" attitude. When Buster Keaton, Rudolph Valentino, Stan Laurel, or Mary Pickford gulped down a Coca-Cola, it was more than a mere endorsement: It also proved to be a guarantee of increased sales! The furnishings, clothing, cigarettes, automobiles—and even soft drinks—used in the unending procession of major motion pictures became the impetus for a new wave of consumerism.

Americans tuned out the self-control portrayed in the media of the 1800s and turned with enthusiasm to new radio broadcasts and silent films. Now, people wanted to be clued in to the latest fashions, learn how to dance the Charleston, and hear about the sexual liberties and scandals of Hollywood stars. This was an age of indulgence, whimsy, and fantasy, and Coca-Cola was just another accessory to help people squeeze as much pleasure out of life as possible. As newspaper columnist Heywood Broun later reported: "The Jazz Age was wicked and monstrous and silly. Unfortunately, I had a good time."

Archie Lee and the Coca-Cola Company seemed to share this sentiment. The consumption of bottled Coke exceeded the volume sold at the soda fountains and sales boomed. By 1929, Coca-Cola had cornered two-thirds of the American soft drink market! As *Soda Pop* author Lawrence Dietz so aptly put it: "The nation was floating in Coke; the Coca-Cola Company was floating in profits."

Unfortunately, the ship of fools was about to sink. On Wednesday, October 30, 1929, the stock market took a dramatic nosedive. "WALL ST. LAYS AN EGG" read the front-page headline in *Variety* as America held its breath.

The Coca-Cola Company, Atlanta, Ga.

AT A COOL AND CHEERFUL PLACE
You'll find a wonderful girl in a real American pose ~ at the soda fountain ~ When thirsty remember her.

RE-FRESH YOURSELF! FIVE CENTS IS THE PRICE

1929

DECEMBER

1929

Sunday	Monday	Tuesday	Wednesday	Thursday	Friday	Saturday
1	2	3	4	5	6	7
8	9	10	11	12	13	14
15	16	17	18	19	20	21
22	23	24	25	26	27	28
29	30	31		Merry Christmas!		

1929 Hayden Hayden

Facing page, left: Artist Hayden Hayden (Howard Renwick) painted this classy image for the 1929 issue of the Coca-Cola calendar. The good times of the Roaring Twenties were about to come to a close. The Depression years that followed saw little if any of the festive spirit portrayed in calendar advertising. *Courtesy of The Coca-Cola Company*

Coca-Cola Bottling Works, 1928

Facing page, right: The beautiful and wholesome "pretty girl" image was always a matter of pride for Asa Candler and the Coca-Cola Company. Since the first inception of the calendar series in 1891, these color-rich lithographs were intended to invoke a quiet sense of elegance and modesty. However, individual bottlers viewed the medium quite differently, and as a result, they produced some interesting (and often risqué) lithos of their own. These unsanctioned calendars of "questionable" taste are extremely popular among collectors and today command top dollar. *Courtesy of The Coca-Cola Company*

1930 Bathing Beauty

Left: Distributed in 1929 prior to the Christmas holiday (and hence the 1929 date shown), this calendar was actually the 1930 model. This would be the last pretty girl image seen on a calendar for the next few years. From 1931 through 1937, Coca-Cola began using more accessible scenes culled from real American life. In light of the Depression and the slow and difficult return to prosperity, these human-interest themes struck a more resonant chord with a nation struggling to get back on its feet. *Courtesy of The Coca-Cola Company*

Chapter 9

"Hey Buddy, Can You Spare a Coke?"

Coca-Cola Survives the Depression

1932 The Old Oaken Bucket

Facing page: In 1932, Norman Rockwell used the same basic "boy and his dog" concept begun one year earlier. This time, the boy's face had changed a bit (he was a bit more handsome) and the dog turned into a beggar. The image wasn't afraid to show what the real soda-sipping customer might be like—even if that meant worn jeans, a tattered straw hat, and bare feet. *Courtesy of The Coca-Cola Company*

Coca-Cola Bottles for Export Ad

Right: During the late 1920s and early 1930s, Coca-Cola's Foreign Department, later known as the Coca-Cola Export Corporation, began to market the famous soft drink brand overseas. As part of the program, designers created a special package known as the Export Bottle to be sold exclusively on ocean liners. This handsome, labeled bottle, which looked as if it contained much more than a mere soda beverage, prompted many overseas operators to inquire about bottling the beverage. *Courtesy of The Coca-Cola Company*

Coca-Cola for Export in bottles!

This delicious and refreshing beverage—pure and sparkling, ready to drink—is now prepared especially for export. In standard split bottles, handsomely labeled and decorated, packed in substantial cases, five dozen bottles to the case. Shipping weight, 85 lbs.

1932 Hayden Hayden Tray
Artist Hayden Hayden painted the image for this 1932 serving tray. Trays produced in the thirties featured a mix of bathing beauties, elegant women, and youthful innocence. As a counterbalance to the scantily clad models, the 1931 tray featured Norman Rockwell's boy and dog. *Courtesy of The Coca-Cola Company*

The Wall Street crash was the start of a severe economic downturn in America's history. The party that had been the twenties was over. The stock market wobbled for a while and then recovered for a brief period. The sudden upswing was a small comfort to those who had lost their life savings and for businesses that could no longer afford employees. But the upswing proved temporary, and things again faltered; businesses closed, people committed suicide, and speculators lost all worldly possessions. The stock of Coca-Cola tumbled.

The crash was only the start. A far more menacing, long-term shadow hovered over America; the crash created a domino effect that would eventually touch the lives of everyone, in one way or another. By 1931, 2,294 banks with deposits of $1.7 billion failed, leaving people without access to their hard-earned savings. Worse yet, the account holders would never be able to recover any of their money from these banks. The crash inspired a permanent distrust for the erstwhile respectable financial community.

According to T. H. Watkins author of *The Great Depression*: "The world of money had not merely failed, it had betrayed an implicit trust. One of cartoonist Rollin Kirby's most effective editorial drawings of 1931 depicted an unemployed man ("Victim of Bank Failure") sitting disconsolately on a park bench. He had so little he couldn't even feed the squirrel sitting in front of him begging for peanuts. 'But why didn't you save some money for the future when times were good?' the squirrel asks. 'I did,' the man replies."

As if things weren't bad enough, years of drought and poor farming practices turned the once-flourishing fields of the south-central United States into dust bowls. The wind carried clouds of dust as far east as New York City where they blocked out the sun and covered everything in the city with a layer of dirt. Having lost everything they had to the drought, farm families packed up and headed to California. John Steinbeck's novel, *The Grapes of Wrath,* aptly described the crushed human spirit behind this exodus after the dust bowl. With all their worldly goods piled onto rusty flivvers, displaced and bedraggled farmers moved west in a motorized version of the wagon train.

The East Coast saw another type of exodus spawned by corporate collapse. In the five months following the crash of the stock market, busi-

nesses failed at the rate of 133 per 10,000. By 1931, the number of corporate failures topped 28,285. Unemployment soared from 1.5 million to 3.2 million, and then to 7.5 million, reaching 12 million by 1932. There was no social security, no central system of charity, and few resources for the respectably unemployed. In order to feed themselves and their young, proud men and women were forced to turn to private charitable organizations for help.

Against this backdrop of bread lines, soup kitchens, poverty, and deprivation, the Coca-Cola Company struggled to survive. Like so many other corporations at the time, the beverage giant was forced to lay off employees. Costs were trimmed to the bone. With a skeleton production crew—and an even smaller office staff—Coca-Cola planned to wait out the storm. The philosophy behind this stance was simple: People could always find a nickel for "the pause that refreshes."

Meanwhile, the number of automobiles on American roads multiplied. Although the Depression caused new car sales to plummet by 75 percent, it did nothing to hinder automobile ownership. Instead of purchasing the latest model Ford, people turned to used models. In 1932, statistics showed that there was one car for every one and a half American families.

In turn, automobile ownership created miles and miles of roads and parkways; eateries, gas stations, and billboards soon followed. According to Christopher Finch author of *Highways to Heaven*, there was a gas station every 895 feet and an eating place every 1,825 feet along the forty-eight-

Migrant Stranded on Route 66
During the days of the Dust Bowl, Americans abandoned nonproductive farms and headed west in search of opportunity. Many followed Route 66 to California, where they planned to work in the fields or take whatever jobs they could find. Unfortunately, things were not much better out West. Many found a hostile reception and were forced to live in camps that exploited those down on their luck. A few never made it to California: Their cars broke down on the desert stretch of Route 66, leaving them stranded. Photo by Dorothea Lange. *National Archives via Coolstock.com*

Al Capone's Soup Kitchen

During the Great Depression, out-of-work men relied on handouts from bread lines and soup kitchens to survive. Here, a group of men wait for a hot meal outside of gangster Al Capone's Chicago, Illinois, soup kitchen. Renowned for his illegal manufacture and distribution of booze during Prohibition, Capone was also quite the philanthropist, putting money back into the community to help those in need. *National Archives via Coolstock.com*

mile stretch of the Boston Post Road. Billboards sprouted up along almost every highway mile. In fact, the stretch of highway between Trenton and Newark, New Jersey, was dotted with more than 500 billboards.

In response to America's newfound mobility, the Coca-Cola Company strove to expand the availability of the bottled product. John C. Staton designed the Icy-O cooler, an appealing advertisement for Coke that made a great point-of-sale display. The cooler's enameled red-and-green trim boasted the familiar Coca-Cola logo on all four sides. In addition, a shelf that was mounted under the cooler held the familiar yellow cases of bottled Coke. But best of all, each cooler held bottles of Coke encased in ice!

By 1930, a mechanically refrigerated cooler made by Glasscock sold for a nearly prohibitive $150. At such a price, few were sold during the Great Depression. The most popular Depression-era cooler was developed in 1934 by Everett Worthington who designed a Coca-Cola cooler with Westinghouse refrigeration (by 1934, the cooling mechanism was also manufactured by Frigidaire). It was the basic box-lid style, painted bright red with the Coca-Cola name in white. It came in five models: three cooled by ice and two by electric refrigeration.

Dealers (as the purchasers of these models were called) loved them. One dealer in Akron, Ohio, stated: "These coolers are responsible for us showing a 200 per cent increase in soft drink sales and have paid for themselves in ice savings alone." Another dealer from Los Angeles, California, testified: "The cooler pays the largest return on its costs of any piece of equipment in my store."

Coca-Cola used proven increased profits, steady sales, and new business to promote these new coolers. As one restaurant owner stated: "I have noticed that many people come into my restaurant after seeing the Coca-Cola cooler out front." While vivid billboards continued to proclaim the refreshing taste of an ice-cold Coke from the roadside, these "silent salesmen" enticed thirsty folks at service stations, grocery stores, and restaurants. This new market exploded in 1936 when the Westinghouse Vendo Top, the first coin-operated machine, took self-service to a new dimension. The Vendo Top gave customers a sense of instant satisfaction and control. Such easy access to their favorite beverage enticed soda drinkers to buy more. This new phenomenon was called "impulse" buying.

Coca-Cola Remembered
By the end of the 1950s, soda machines were available in all shapes and sizes. In business for over twenty-four years, Cavalier supplied many of those machines to the retailer—bringing the convenience of buying a cold Coca-Cola at a moment's notice to anyone with a pocket full of change. *Courtesy of The Coca-Cola Company*

Meanwhile, hard times caused a diametric shift in the Coca-Cola Company's calendar images. Before the Great Depression, images of pretty girls graced the calendars. But by 1931, idyllic scenes painted by Norman Rockwell, N. C. Wyeth, and Frederick Stanley replaced the fair maidens. Rockwell's paintings appealed to childhood memories, a common bond everyone shared. The 1931 "Tom Sawyer" calendar depicted the fun of enjoying the simple things in life: good food, simple surroundings, the companionship of a dog, and an ice-cold Coke. In a time when so few lived comfortably, Rockwell's canvases were appealing.

Prior to the Great Depression, Coca-Cola calendars and serving trays featured identical images. During the Depression, although Coca-Cola did feature the popular Tom Sawyer image on the 1931 serving tray, the trays continued to feature images of beautiful women, many of whom wore swimsuits. The swimsuit of the Depression era was a svelte little number, complete with bustline and waist. Unlike the pantaloon and swimskirt bathing suits that they replaced, new swimsuit designs enhanced the female figure, spurring the American media to publish a wave of bathing-beauty photographs.

In this same spirit, film stars posed in the flimsy bathing suits. As emissaries of goodwill, stars appeared to be full of jocular mischief. The "screwball" comedies of the thirties gave the stars a platform for delivering a little comic relief to the often-weary public. The Coca-Cola Company quickly employed such actors as Clark Gable, Claudette Colbert, Joan Crawford, Cary Grant, Jackie Cooper, and Jean Harlowe to endorse Coca-Cola.

1931 Norman Rockwell Boy

Above: Known by collectors as the "Tom Sawyer" image, artist Norman Rockwell captured the spirit of rural America and the promise of youth in this 1931 calendar image. At the time, the nation was feeling the effects of the Great Depression, and images such as this brought everyone back down to earth. It was more likely that average Americans—no doubt down on their luck—could relate to this engaging motif than to a primped-up society girl attending a party. *Courtesy of The Coca-Cola Company*

1933 Frederic Stanley

Right: Artist Frederic Stanley followed Rockwell's lead with the 1933 calendar image, "The Village Blacksmith." Here was the real workingman's America. You could smell the fire, feel the breeze, and imagine what it was like to enjoy a Coke during those simple times of school, suspenders, and slingshots. Stanley was a rival of Norman Rockwell and gained widespread notoriety with *Saturday Evening Post* covers. *Courtesy of The Coca-Cola Company*

"How about a Coke"

Coca-Cola shunned anything that might reveal the dark side of the Great Depression. It was important to keep the public's mind focused on happier days. To this end, advertising featured gainfully employed men and women enjoying "The Pause That Refreshes." In a fortunate twist of fate, the Depression did create better working conditions for the American workforce. Organized labor pushed the government to pass new laws that guaranteed employees weekends off to spend with their families, vacations, lunch breaks, and the much-needed work break. The Coca-Cola slogan "The Pause That Refreshes" took on a whole new meaning as newly liberated employees gave each other a nod and a wink while reaching for an ice-cold Coke!

The Depression also gave birth to other symbols of optimism, the most notable being the image of the Santa Claus that we know and love today. The Coca-Cola Company's Santa Claus debuted in the December 1930 issue of the *Ladies' Home Journal.* The headline states: "The busiest man in the world comes up smiling after . . . 'the pause that refreshes.'" The ad features Santa in a busy department store soda fountain, surrounded by starry-eyed children. Presumably taking a break from delivering gifts, Santa gulps down an ice-cold Coke. The copy reads, "Even Old Santa, busiest man in the world, devotes a minute now and then to 'the pause that refreshes.'"

Yet this department store Santa—in all his regalia—could not hold a candle to the embodiment of jolly good humor that Haddon Sundblom illustrated for Coca-Cola in 1931. Sundblom wanted to create a Santa that would be the epitome of someone lovable, someone you could hug and share secrets with. And, his round face and belly were only part of the picture. Sundblom wanted to make Santa realistic, yet a little bit mysteri-

How About a Coke Blotter, 1934
This Coca-Cola blotter of 1934 featured three fresh-faced girls, looking much like the Andrews Sisters and other girl groups that captured the scene during the 1930s. It's a wonder that the models are still smiling: Only one year earlier, competitor Pepsi-Cola lowered the price of its twelve-ounce drink from ten to five cents. *Preziosi, Coolstock.com*

It had to be good to get where it is

World's largest soda fountain in the great department store of Famous-Barr Co., St. Louis, where busy Christmas shoppers pause and refresh themselves with ice-cold Coca-Cola.

Drink
Coca-Cola
Delicious and Refreshing

THE BUSIEST MAN IN THE WORLD
comes up smiling
after... *the pause that refreshes*

RSE you find wonderful soda ains in the great department n Old Santa, busiest man in the otes a minute now and then to at refreshes. It's a happy, socia- Christmas shopping—a little est and refreshment that gives start. •• *The pause that refreshes,*

as everyone knows, is the short time it takes to enjoy an ice-cold Coca-Cola. The busier you are the more important it becomes. You relax, take a deep breath and quench your thirst with the tingling deliciousness of this pure drink of natural flavors. And, like Santa Claus himself, you come up smiling.

THE BEST SERVED DRINK IN THE WORLD
A pure drink of natural flavors served ice-cold in its own glass and in its own bottle: The crystal-thin Coca-Cola glass that represents the best in soda fountain service. The distinctive Coca-Cola bottle you can always identify; it is sterilized, filled and sealed air-tight without the touch of human hands, insuring purity and wholesomeness. The Coca-Cola Company, Atlanta, Ga.

LISTEN IN ⟿ Grantland Rice ⟿ Famous Sports Champions ⟿ Coca-Cola Orchestra ⟿ Wed. 10:30 to 11 p. m. Eastern Standard Time ⟿ Coast to Coast N B C Network ⟿

mpany, 1930   N I N E   M I L L I O N   A   D A Y

Coke's First Santa Claus
Facing page: In December 1930, the *Ladies' Home Journal* debuted a full-page advertisement featuring Coca-Cola's first Santa Claus. A delicious and refreshing Coke always made Old Santa smile. And you can bet the kids took notice! *Courtesy of The Coca-Cola Company*

The Pause That Refreshes, 1932
Above: When Coca-Cola used the slogan "The Pause That Refreshes" during the early 1930s, this play-on-words (or play-on-slogan, if you will) Santa Claus advertisement appeared in national publications. *Courtesy of The Coca-Cola Company*

Santa Claus Saturday Evening Post
Left: The image of St. Nicholas, the patron saint of children from Asia Minor (circa A.D. 300) was transformed in 1844 when poet Clement Clark Moore published *'Twas the Night Before Christmas*. Describing Santa as a "plump, jolly old elf," his work influenced artists for the next fifty years, causing them to paint Santa Claus as a gnome-like creature! By the turn of the century, confusion reigned as Christmas cards imported from Europe didn't adhere to Moore's imagery. In 1931, artist Haddon Sundblom began working for Coca-Cola and set upon the task of focusing the Santa image for a Christmas ad campaign. The result was the rotund, happy, red-suited, white-bearded, black-booted, North Pole stereotype we all know and love as Santa Claus today. *Coolstock.com Advertising Archives*

ous, as well. And although very few children expected Santa to give them gifts during the Depression, his presence gave them hope.

By 1932, ads featured a surprised Santa who had just discovered a bottle of Coke and a glass on the mantel. A child's scribbled note summed up what many kids were hoping: "Dear Santa, please PAUSE here—Jimmy." From that point on, Sundblom's Santa Claus, Coke, and children were intrinsically linked.

The famous Sundblom Santa also graced the new Coca-Cola take-home carton, developed in December 1931. (The first Coca-Cola six-bottle

carton was patented on September 23, 1924.) It was the company's tactic to encourage homemakers to use this portable cardboard box as a handy carrying tool. The customer would purchase six bottles of Coke and place the bottles in the box, saving the container for the next trip to the store. Imprinted on the carton, the slogan "6 bottles of tingling refreshment" caused many Coca-Cola lovers to pick one up, but it wasn't until the mid 1930s that these portable six packs really caught on with the public.

This turnabout can be attributed to another new phenomenon that emerged during the thirties: the supermarket. Born of necessity, the self-service grocery store was a way for the grocer to cut back on expenses by eliminating clerks and allowing the customer to do their own shopping. At the time, there was plenty of cheap rental space available in large buildings. The first of these big markets opened up on Jamaica Avenue in Queens, New York, in 1930. King Kullen was packed with truckloads of groceries purchased at reduced prices, and the savings were passed on to the customer.

It didn't take long for these bargain grocery stores to become popular with the budget-minded public. By the mid thirties, the first chain stores—such as A&P—were doing grand business. The rows and rows of grocery products stacked high created the need for another marketing innovation: colorful packaging. This also proved to be the start of a new era for the Coca-Cola Company: an era when they began to target the housewife and encourage her to buy Coke in large quantities.

In order to jump-start this buying habit, the Coca-Cola Company had to educate America's homemakers on the advantages of keeping the pantry well-stocked with Coke. Radio media reached the highest number of women in the shortest amount of time, so Coca-Cola chose Ida Bailey Allen—founder of The National Radio Home-maker's Club—to deliver its

Hot Lunch Sandwiches

During the 1930s, even small towns like Tonkawa, Oklahoma, were rife with soda pop advertising. In this Farm Security Administration photo, two local cafes offer the best of both worlds: the local favorite Dr Pepper, and the all-around favorite Coca-Cola. It's interesting to note that the "Pause . . . Drink" slogan is not recorded as being an official advertising line. More than likely, it was a variation of a theme adapted by a local bottler or merchant. "Pause . . . Go Refreshed" was rolled out in 1944. *Library of Congress via Coolstock.com*

1935 Rockwell Tom Sawyer

Top: Perhaps America's most beloved illustrator of the twentieth century, Norman Rockwell (1894–1978) is known worldwide for his honest depiction of daily life in small-town and rural America. Indeed, Rockwell's idyllic world is a glimpse of America's best—a world populated by Boy Scouts, shopkeepers, mothers, children, grandpas, and grandmas. Rockwell wanted to create an ideal America in his paintings and stuck to his convictions. In his best-selling 1960 biography, *My Adventures as an Illustrator,* he wrote: "I paint life as I would like it to be." *Courtesy of The Coca-Cola Company*

1936 Wyeth at the Sea

Middle: N. C. Wyeth captured the essence of seaside splendor in this 1936 Coca-Cola calendar art painting. This was the year of Coca-Cola's fiftieth anniversary, and the company wasn't ashamed to promote the achievement. Born in Needham, Massachusetts, N. C. Wyeth became one of the foremost book illustrators and mural painters in America in the early part of the twentieth century. The first painting he sold was of a wild bucking bronco, an image that gained a national audience as the *Saturday Evening Post* cover of February 21, 1903. *Courtesy of The Coca-Cola Company*

N. C. Wyeth 1937 Calendar

Bottom: A boy, his dog, and two bottles of Coca-Cola—what else could a young man want? Is the young lad off to his favorite fishing hole to enjoy both bottles by himself, or to meet a friend? Only artist N. C. Wyeth, painter of this 1937 Coca-Cola calendar image, knows for sure. A longtime resident of remote, fog-shrouded Monhegan Island, Maine, artist Wyeth had many opportunities to paint such pastoral scenes. *Courtesy of The Coca-Cola Company*

At War With Pepsi

During the Great Depression, the Pepsi-Cola Company, longtime competitor of and cola second-fiddle to Coca-Cola, was doing all that it could to siphon off some of the tremendous profits enjoyed by the Coca-Cola Company.

Invented by pharmacist Caleb Bradham in New Bern, North Carolina, in 1893, Pepsi-Cola's history closely paralleled that of Coca-Cola. But Pepsi was one of the many soda companies that went belly up during the sugar crisis. After Pepsi declared bankruptcy in March 1923, Coca-Cola never believed the drink would someday be back to haunt them. But that's just what happened. Roy Megargel bought the Pepsi trademark from Bradham and managed to keep the soft drink business afloat until the stock market crash, when he sold to Charles Guth. Guth owned a chain of fountains in the Northeast, which served as perfect venues for Pepsi-Cola.

By the mid 1930s, the company reaped profits of two million dollars. Every year, Pepsi-Cola gained more and more of a foothold in the domestic and overseas markets, giving Coca-Cola a run for its money.

Pepsi fired the first shot in the "cola wars" in 1933 when they came out with a twelve-ounce bottle of cola that sold for only five cents. Citizens who were already low on cash gave the low-priced soda their seal of approval. At last, there was a flavorful alternative to Coke that was a lot easier on the pocketbook. With this move, Pepsi-Cola established itself as a serious competitor for Coca-Cola's share of the cola-drinking market.

Tempty . . . Tasty, Circa 1941
In support of America's war effort, Pepsi-Cola changed the color of its bottle crowns to red, white, and blue in 1941. A Pepsi canteen located in Times Square, New York, operated throughout the war years enabling more than a million families to record messages for armed service personnel overseas. *Preziosi, Coolstock.com*

1934 Father and Daughter

A father and daughter of the Southern plantation scene were the subjects for this 1934 calendar image by Norman Rockwell. As an artist, he was perfectly suited for the assignment: In addition to his work for Coca-Cola, he executed major book commissions that included a new edition of Tom Sawyer and a biography of Louisa May Alcott. *Courtesy of The Coca-Cola Company*

advertising message. As Ida recited in her introduction to *One Hundred Four Prize Radio Recipes*: "There are twenty million of us—Home-Makers. That is our job." D'Arcy was quick to exploit Ida's influence on American women. Soon, Ida offered over the radio, a new booklet called *When you Entertain—What to do, and How.* The booklet answered all the questions a good hostess posed. Mrs. Allen's universal answer to questions about refreshment was an ice-cold Coke!

The thirties ushered in a new age of radio advertising. After all, radio broadcasting was now an accepted part of American culture. The big bands, radio serials, and zany comedies were all products of the Great Depression. Radio had become a portal to the world. To many people, radio was not only a source of information, it was a friend and a constant companion. And advertisers were careful not to invade the listener's privacy. Advertising was a part of the radio show, and sponsorship was the avenue through which products were introduced to the audience. All ads, done in a friendly, informative tone, appeared to enhance programs.

1938 Coca-Cola Tray
Manufactured by American Art Works, of Conshoctin, Ohio, this 1938 Coca-Cola serving tray echoes the early pretty girl motif seen so often in the company's promotional materials. By the 1950s, the picturesque pose with generic background gave way to a more realistic image of a pretty girl in a variety of situations and environments. *Courtesy of The Coca-Cola Company*

Under D'Arcy's direction, the Coca-Cola Company sponsored many radio programs. The *Pause that Refreshes on the Air*, a half-hour musical program that featured a sixty-five-piece orchestra and a twenty-five-member vocal group, stands out above the rest. Dr. Frank Black, the distinguished musical director of NBC during the 1934–35 season, directed the show. *Pause that Refreshes on the Air* was unique for its time because musicians played selections without interruption for fourteen minutes a stretch. A commercial announcement aired at the beginning, middle, and end of the show. Shows such as this made radio the main target for national advertising campaigns.

Nationwide broadcasts promoted Coca-Cola from coast to coast, and the American people responded, filling their glasses and refrigerators with ice-cold Coca-Cola. Despite the Depression, Coca-Cola sales were on the rise, and soon the phrase "as American as Coca-Cola" had a life of its own. By the end of the thirties, Coke had achieved the enviable rank as *the* national beverage, the great American drink.

Rockford Aluminum Carton

Left: Manufactured by the J. L. Clark Manufacturing Company of Rockford, Illinois, the aluminum carton was a handy accessory for the housewife who wanted to transport her Coke efficiently. It may seem curious today to make a big deal about an aluminum carton, unless one knows that early Coca-Cola bottles were sold individually or in large wooden cases that had to be returned. The personal Coke caddie allowed consumers to pick up a half-dozen bottles and transport them with relative ease. *Coolstock.com Advertising Archives*

Cold Refreshment Blotter, 1937

Below: Whenever possible, Coca-Cola liked to advertise on products that were useful to the customer. The paper blotter was one such item, handy when writing with the fountain pens indicative of the day. Today, blotters are an affordable option for the collector who wishes to gather a wide variety of images and slogans pertaining to the Coca-Cola brand. *Preziosi, Coolstock.com*

"Here's the way to feel refreshed"

Coca-Cola has the charm of purity. It is prepared with the finished art that comes from a lifetime of practice. Its delicious taste never loses the freshness of appeal that first delighted you...always bringing you a cool, clean sense of complete refreshment. Thirst asks nothing more.

Take hold of an ice-cold bottle of Coca-Cola and you have the whole answer to thirst in the palm of your hand. Lift it to your lips and drink. You'll find out at once what *the pause that refreshes* with ice-cold Coca-Cola can really mean...to you. Try it.

Drink

Coca-Cola

TRADE MARK REG. U.S. PAT. OFF.

Delicious and Refreshing

5¢

The World Goes Crazy For Coke

Coca-Cola Gains a Worldwide Audience

Feel Refreshed Ad, 1940

Facing page: "Here's the way to feel refreshed" was a slogan that caught the eye of magazine readers in 1940. That year, German troops unleashed Blitzkrieg, overrunning Holland and Belgium, and parts of France. Popular singers called "crooners," included Frank Sinatra, Bing Crosby, Dinah Shore, and Perry Como. The four-wheel-drive vehicle known as the Jeep was introduced, and the patent for the first photocopying machine was issued (later manufactured by Xerox). *Coolstock.com Advertising Archives*

Your Thirst Takes Wings

Right: While a woman was depicted wearing a flight suit in this 1941 calendar image, the truth is that most of America's women remained at home during the war effort. Nevertheless, they rose to the occasion, with many working in factories to produce airplanes, bombs, and other weapons of war. "Your thirst takes wings when you treat it to an ice-cold Coca-Cola" was actually the slogan used in 1940. A version of this calendar was also produced for the French Canadian market. *Courtesy of The Coca-Cola Company*

When the Japanese bombed Pearl Harbor in 1941, the once-remote World War II hit American soil. With the war on its doorstep, America was no longer joining the fight just to help its allies—the war had become a personal conflict. America shook off its apathy and faced the enemy with passion and courage. Men, women, and children joined the fight against the enemy, either on the front or at home.

During the 1940s, patriotism fueled the advertising campaigns. The Coca-Cola Company began to dream up ways to support the war effort while making efficient use of its advertising dollars. In 1941, one particular Coke ad addressed the time of crisis in America and commented on how citizens must stay fit to "avoid the tensions that lower efficiency." Advertising copywriters went so far as to suggest that drinking Coca-Cola was an important part of a fitness regiment. Many things contribute to fitness, copywriters penned: "One of them is the pause that refreshes with ice-cold Coca-Cola."

In 1942, Coca-Cola began to imply in its ads that it could somehow contribute to a larger cause, namely, the war effort. That same year, the "Work Refreshed" slogan debuted in ads showing defense plant workers—including former housewives—working hard to support the ongoing war effort. Now, Coca-Cola was more than just a soft drink, it was also an accessory that Americans needed to stay ahead and maintain peak performance. If workers drank Coke, the message implied, they would be able to work more efficiently. "Rosie the Riveter" (a nickname given to the female worker after her depiction on the May 29, 1943, cover of the *Saturday Evening Post*) relied on Coke to stay alert. Who wouldn't want to use a product that could help the nation win the war?

Coca-Cola During War Time
During World War II, American girls waited patiently for their husbands and boyfriends to return home. In turn, the soldiers longed for jukeboxes, a hamburger, and sharing an ice-cold Coca-Cola with their favorite gal. Those fortunate enough to receive curvy bottles in "care packages" from home became celebrities on the front. An unopened Coca-Cola bottle was in such high demand that it could easily fetch one hundred dollars! The worldwide market for Coca-Cola was unfolding. By the end of the war, Coke was primed for its global debut. *Courtesy of The Coca-Cola Company*

LITHO IN U. S. A.   COPYRIGHT MCMXLII THE COCA-COLA COMPANY

As the conflict in Europe raged on, Coca-Cola continued to bottle its product in thirty-five allied and neutral nations. In many regions overseas, America's fighting force could still find a bottle of Coke. For those who had to do without, salvation came on June 29, 1943, when General Dwight D. Eisenhower sent a message to officials in the United States from the Allied Headquarters in North Africa. It read: "On early convoy request shipment three million bottled Coca-Cola (filled) and complete equipment for bottling, washing, capping same quantity twice monthly." The urgency was clear, it would take Coca-Cola to boost the morale of our soldiers and motivate them to win the war.

By this time, Coke was a tried and true icon of American culture. As many letters from servicemen attested, Coca-Cola was part of the American dream.

Completely Refreshing

"Completely Refreshing" was the slogan used in 1941 and the theme for this Coca-Cola blotter. In the days before ballpoint pens and inexpensive markers, businessmen used fountain pens to write. Sometimes, the ink took a while to dry, so writers pressed blotters against the paper to soak up the excess ink and prepare a letter for the post. Today, unused blotters are highly collectible and a favorite among all Coke aficionados. *Preziosi, Coolstock.com*

Atlanta Coca-Cola Building

By the 1940s, the Coca-Cola Company building in Atlanta, Georgia, exhibited the same stately grandeur of any other large business of the day. The production of soda water was now mainstream and the entities that manufactured it just another part of the Fortune 500. *Preziosi, Coolstock.com*

Ihre Zukunft Coke Ad
Right: "Your Future in the Coca-Cola Business" was an ad slogan printed in German trade periodicals during the early campaign to promote the spread of Coca-Cola worldwide. *Courtesy of The Coca-Cola Company*

Katzenjammer Coke
Bottom: The sentiment in this German Coca-Cola advertisement is equal to a 1927 American version that states: "For that tired, discouraged feeling—drink Coca-Cola." What it really means is that an ice-cold Coca-Cola is a great remedy for a hangover! *Courtesy of The Coca-Cola Company*

Many a serviceman stationed thousands of miles from home longed for a cold, icy bottle of Coca-Cola. For some, merely having a bottle of Coke to look at was enough to bolster morale. Many anticipated "red letter day," the day when letters from home arrived, accompanied by precious bottles of Coca-Cola. Within those familiar bottles was the true embodiment of freedom, "a little piece of home."

Many stories that demonstrated how much Coca-Cola meant to Americans emerged from the war. War correspondent Ernie Pyle wrote an article about a GI in Italy who raffled off a single bottle of Coke for the tidy sum of four thousand dollars. Organized to help the survivors of soldiers killed in action, the gesture showed just how important the drink had become. Empty Coke bottles were used for all sorts of things—as insulators, as bombs to deflate the tires of Japanese aircraft, and as weapons.

After the war ended, the time of sacrifice came to a close. By the 1950s, prosperity was on its way back in America—good news for the manufacturers of products like soft drinks. Now, when it came to personal refreshment, cola lovers no longer required "twice as much for a nickel." The concept of frugality was just one more thing that reminded people of the hardships endured during the war. Everyone wanted, even demanded, the quality of Coca-Cola—and didn't mind paying a higher price for it.

During the war, American GIs had introduced Coca-Cola to people around the world, without Coca-Cola spending a cent. The Coca-Cola bottling plants now scattered around the world became the starting point for a worldwide expansion and the beginning of a new era. Germany, Japan, and other former foes would soon all fall under the influence of Coca-Cola!

Eiskalt Coke Sprite Boy
Around 1940, artist Haddon Sundblom used his own face as a model in order to revamp a Walt Disney version of the elfin face known as "Sprite." Unfortunately, the public nicknamed the little imp "Cokie," something that was frowned upon by Coca-Cola's legal department (who feared it would lead to trademark problems, not to mention the negative associations with cocaine that the name conjured up). As a result, Sprite was quietly retired, popping up for an occasional appearance during special promotions. *Eiskalt,* or "ice-cold" were the words that accompanied his smiling face in German ads of the time period. *Courtesy of The Coca-Cola Company*

THEY
ALL
STOP
TO BUY

Coca-Cola Cooler Brochure
During the 1940s, Coca-Cola distributed sales brochures advertising their latest line of refrigerated coolers. The cover featured fans of the soft drink happily consuming the beverage. Inside, text and photographs detailed the cooler's operating parameters and technical information. *Courtesy of Larry Schulz*

Globalization didn't take long. On May 15, 1950, *Time* magazine featured the Coca-Cola Company in a cover story. The memorable cover illustration depicted an animated, smiling red disk feeding a bottle of Coke to what looked to be a very pleased globe (characterized by raised eyebrows, a satisfied grin, and serene eyes). By the early 1950s, more than one-quarter of Coca-Cola sales were in foreign markets. Coca-Cola *had* gone global.

Nevertheless, there was still much work to be done at home to protect the fickle market from increasing competition. Advertising on the brave new format of television became the best way to capture the attention of America's soda sippers. It wasn't long before flickering cathode-ray tubes were trumpeting the virtues of Coke across the nation. Viewers from coast to coast were pulling up easy chairs and TV trays to see the show.

In 1950, Coca-Cola sponsored its first television program. The Thanksgiving special, starring Edgar Bergen and Charlie McCarthy, was the very first live network TV show. In December 1950, a Walt Disney Christmas special followed, pairing the national appeal of Disney characters with the Coca-Cola drink.

As the post-war economic boom of the 1950s reshaped America, the public's appetite for everything increased. The race to super-size began in 1955, when Coke replaced the meager six-and-one-half-ounce bottle with ten-ounce king-sized and twenty-six-ounce family-sized bottles. The

Délicieux Coca-Cola Ad
American advertisements of the 1940s and 1950s that featured people enjoying leisurely activities—such as playing tennis—were duplicated for many of the Coca-Cola Company's foreign markets. Like other nations, the citizens of France were informed of the "Delicious" qualities of the Coca-Cola beverage with simple words and colorful images. *Courtesy of The Coca-Cola Company*

impetus here was price point, not convenience. Due to rising costs, the company could no longer hold the six-and-one-half-ounce-sized Coke at five cents. Yet, it was awkward to raise the price without increasing the size.

Meanwhile, the patrons at lunch counters and soda fountains were offered a larger portion of Coke, too. Here, customers could buy a twelve-ounce glass and pay twice the price. And in 1950, the Coca-Cola Company test-marketed twelve-ounce metal containers with flip-top lids in California and New England. The new portable containers were a huge hit with Cola fans who could now take their favorite beverage anywhere.

The fifties brought changes on the advertising front, too. When marketing guru Archie Lee passed away in 1950, the D'Arcy Advertising Agency

Drive Refreshed

Right: "Along the highway to anywhere" was the Coke slogan of 1949. One year later, this Coke ad appeared in several national periodicals, including *National Geographic*. At long last, Coke was available just about everywhere, including many of the nation's service stations and roadside businesses. It's interesting to note that by the late 1940s, the Coca-Cola Company's obsession with the public asking for the product by its official name had eased. Now, both "Coke" and "Coca-Cola" were acceptable. *Coolstock.com Advertising Archives*

Yes Girl 1946 Poster

Bottom: "Yes!" Here's an example of printed Coca-Cola advertising in its most pure and simple form. No slogans, no play on words, no ambiguity—just a pretty girl in a bathing suit and one single word. The message is clear: Yes, I want a Coke. Produced in 1946, this poster won first place and a grand-prize medal in a contest sponsored by the outdoor advertising industry. *Courtesy of The Coca-Cola Company*

lost its creative fizz. This did not bode well for the Coca-Cola campaign. In 1955, *Business Week* reported that industry insiders were mocking Coca-Cola's current ad campaign, claiming that it resembled Pepsi's. On March 31, 1956, the Coca-Cola Company hired the McCann-Erickson advertising agency to replace D'Arcy.

During the early 1950s the D'Arcy Agency had begun to replace illustrated ads with color photography, and the result was disastrous—skin tones appeared orange, giving women an unattractive, jaundiced look. When McCann-Erickson took over the advertising account, the agency immediately began experimenting with still-life photography and found that film captured food far better than people. A plethora of still-life images followed, featuring frosty bottles and beaded glasses alongside stacked sandwiches and pizza wedges.

Although the ads were pleasing to the eye, they did not move people to buy. By 1959, Pepsi-Cola had secured more than a third of the national cola market. Furthermore, in the early 1960s Pepsi's ad campaign portrayed Coca-Cola as the drink of the World War II generation, and Pepsi as the drink of their children ("Pepsi Generation"). McCann-Erickson spent a staggering $53 million to counter this impression, putting their "Things go better with Coke" ads into magazines, on television, and on the radio. As a result, Coke became the most heavily advertised product in the country.

The cola ad wars continued over the television airwaves during the 1960s. This time, celebrity singers were all the rage, and the Coca-Cola Company secured the services of industry notables such as Connie Francis, Nancy Sinatra, Tom Jones, and the Supremes. To up the ante, Coca-Cola added a few new soft drinks to its repertoire. Sprite, Fanta, and Fresca appealed to soda drinkers who craved something other than the standard cola fare. And Coca-Cola introduced Tab to nab the weight-conscious market.

In 1970 as the controversial Vietnam War raged, the McCann-Erickson ad agency debuted a TV commercial featuring young people from around the world holding hands and singing: "I'd like to buy the world a Coke." With this overwhelmingly popular ad, the Coca-Cola Company linked drinking Coke with peace, love, and harmony. The song became so popular that Coca-Cola sold more than one million records featuring the noncommercial version of the jingle, proving once again that their product is "The Real Thing." The seventies also ushered in two more Coca-Cola products, Mr. Pibb and Mello Yello.

During the 1980s, Pepsi had signed such notables as Michael Jackson and Madonna to endorse their product. Coca-Cola followed suit,

1948 Coca-Cola Calendar
The Betty Grable look—featuring the short-banged hairstyle of the day—graced the Coca-Cola calendar in 1948. That year "Everybody likes to work refreshed" and "Think of lunch time as refreshment time" were two of the latest Coca-Cola slogans. During the economic boom of the post-war years, people needed inspiration to keep going at the frenetic pace. *Courtesy of The Coca-Cola Company*

1950 Serving Tray
Formerly (and inaccurately) known as the 1948 tray by collectors, this 1950 model exhibits all of the exuberance of the post-war era. At long last, Americans were ready to kick up their heels and enjoy the prosperity they had put off for so many years. This tray was the first one produced after the war. *Courtesy of The Coca-Cola Company*

signing Michael Jordan, New Kids on the Block, Elton John, Aretha Franklin, and Paula Abdul.

Unfortunately, no celebrity could counter the effects of the Pepsi Challenge taste tests. In malls and other such venues across the nation, Pepsi challenged cola drinkers to take a sip of Pepsi and a sample of Coke, without knowing which soda was which, and decide which they liked best. Time after time, Coke found itself the loser. In 1985, the Coca-Cola Company took drastic action, changing the formula of their drink! On April 23, 1985, the Coca-Cola Company announced the change at a press conference in Atlanta. The company hired comedian Bill Cosby as the television pitchman who introduced the product to a stunned America.

Much to the Coca-Cola Company's chagrin, angry consumers vehemently opposed the new product and demanded the old Coke formula be returned. Only seventy-eight days after the New Coke had been introduced "Classic Coke" was resurrected and sold right alongside the new formula. The tactic to change America's beloved Coke formula resulted in a market share tumble; shares went from a high of 15 percent to a frightening low of 1.4 percent. Shortly thereafter, New Coke disappeared from store shelves. Not one to stop trying new things, the Coca-Cola Company filled that empty shelf space with two new products—Diet Coke and Cherry Coke.

By the mid 1990s, the cola wars raged on. But the drink that was once a luxury had finally replaced water as the drink of choice. Men, women, and children—it seemed that everyone was downing soda pop. Coca-Cola and a variety of other sodas had become an American staple.

Coca-Cola has definitely come full circle. Although it is no longer a medicine for the body, drinking a Coca-Cola in the afternoon seems to provide just the pick-me-up workers around the world need to finish the day. And, judging from the popularity of collecting the old Coca-Cola serving trays, coolers, signs, and advertisements that introduced Coca-Cola to the American public long ago, it's clear that Coca-Cola is here to stay.

Designed for Hospitality Ad, 1949
In 1876, paying seventy-five dollars for a piece of bottle-washing equipment was viewed by the industry as outlandish! By 1965, even though the cost of a basic bottle washer skyrocketed to eighty thousand dollars, attitudes changed. With the capacity to wash five hundred bottles per minute, bottlers found that it was easy to cycle through the returns and restock the shelves as quickly as possible. Without ample resources to clean and process bottles, the high-volume sales promoted in take-it-home ads like this one would not have been possible.
Coolstock.com Advertising Archives

What You Want Is a Coke

Above: In 1952, Americans were enjoying life and the great outdoors. Coca-Cola was part of the scene, an accessory, if you will, of the good life. Ads featured the new slogans "The upper hand on thirst" and "What you want is a Coke." *Coolstock.com Advertising Archives*

Vendo V-44 Coca-Cola Machine

Left: Introduced in 1956, the thin Vendo V-44 model vending machine decked out in classic red and white Coca-Cola colors is one of the most sought-after machines today. Capable of dispensing a total of forty-four bottles, it's a favorite among the many newcomers to the hobby of soda machine collectibles. Fully restored, an attractive "44" can sell for close to three thousand dollars. ©2001 *Mike Witzel, Coolstock.com*

You Taste Its Quality Ad

Facing page: Ads like this one from 1951 promoted Coke as a drink with wholesome goodness. Taste was equated with quality and the health claims of the earlier years faded away. Having a good time—with taste in mind—was more important to consumers than any actual benefits a product might have. This was the 1950s—a decade to enjoy life. *Coolstock.com Advertising Archives*

You taste its quality

**Quality means
wholesome goodness,
and Coca-Cola is just that.**

Drink
Coca-Cola
REG. U.S. PAT. OFF.
5¢

1950 Bottles on a Tray Calendar

Above: During the early 1950s, Coca-Cola advertising took a whole new direction: domestic accessibility. The new idea was that consumers should buy an entire six pack (or more) of the drink and bring it home. Coca-Cola was no longer just a treat for Sunday outings or trips into town. It was an everyday beverage that mom could stock in the family refrigerator and bring out on a silver platter whenever guests dropped in. Having no Coke in the Frigidaire was equal to having no sense of hospitality. *Courtesy of The Coca-Cola Company*

1957 Skier Girl

Right: "The pause that refreshes" is perhaps one of the most memorable Coca-Cola advertising slogans of all time. Whether it was skiing, swimming, biking, or hiking—Coke was promoted as the soft drink to relieve your thirst and get you going on your way, refreshed and energized. *Courtesy of The Coca-Cola Company*

1956 Beach Girl
"Refreshment through 70 years" was the counterbalancing slogan to this 1956 "There's nothing like a Coke" calendar image. Here, the model wears the latest designer swimwear, a stark contrast to the dowdy "Princess-cut" suit (blouse and pants all in one piece) the girl is wearing in the inset image. During the 1950s, clothing designer Christian Dior introduced the relaxed-silhouette sack, trapeze, A-line, and Y-line. *Courtesy of The Coca-Cola Company*

Sprite Boy Blotter

Above: In 1953, the Coca-Cola Sprite boy popped up and made his appearance on advertising blotters. This was a banner year for the Coca-Cola ad men and new slogans. Maybe you remember "Delicious, sparkling, always refreshing"; "Dependable as sunrise"; "Favored above all others for refreshment"; "Midsummer magic"; "The refreshment of friends"; or "Hospitality at its best"? All were Coca-Cola slogans rolled out during that year. *Coolstock.com Advertising Archives*

Convertible Teen, 1954

Right: Jessie Kirby and R. W. Jackson built America's first drive-in restaurant, called the "Pig Stand," in Dallas, Texas, in 1921. Savvy operators liked the "Pig Stand" format and copied it. By the 1950s, eating in your car was a national craze. Curbside stands were everywhere and soft drinks like Coca-Cola were accepted as the perfect companion for hand-held foods and for enjoying while out on a cruise. *Coolstock.com Advertising Archives*

refreshes you best!
SAY THE M'GUIRE SISTERS

DRINK Coca-Cola IN BOTTLES

Thirst asks nothing more

Coca-Cola DRINK

Yes sir, everybody knows
ice-cold Coca-Cola
is delicious and refreshing.

DRINK Coca-Cola ICE COLD

The McGuire Sisters
Top: The McGuire Sisters (Phyllis, Dorothy, and Christine) got their big break on the *Arthur Godfrey Talent Show*. They replaced a group known as the Chordettes and entertained the home audience for six years. The trio recorded many hits throughout the 1950s and 1960s, including "Do You Remember When," "Somebody Loves Me," "Moonglow," and "Sincerely." The sisters leveraged their immense popularity to promote Coca-Cola, making history by receiving the highest payment for advertising up to that time. *Preziosi, Coolstock.com*

Thirst Asks Nothing More Ad, 1951
Left: What better image than one of our servicemen enjoying an ice-cold bottle of Coke to promote something that delivers pure happiness in bottled form? In 1951, America was deeply involved in the Korean War, and the military man once again became the focus of the American public. At home, on leave, and on base, Army, Navy, Air Force, and Marine servicemen enjoyed a frosty bottle whenever they could. *Courtesy of Rebecca Mastoras, Coolstock. com Advertising Archives*

Aretha Franklin Pop Art Poster

Singer Aretha Franklin, a musical artist known for hits such as "Chain of Fools" and "Respect," was the inspiration behind this Coca-Cola pop art ad of 1968. The tastes of young Coca-Cola fans were changing, and the sentimental images of the Rockwell years were no longer effective. Now, the psychedelic colors of the pop art scene caught one's eye. What a deal: For a mere fifty cents, fans received a 16-by-27-inch poster for a "very vertical place of honor." *Coolstock.com Advertising Archives*

The Beatles Drink Coca-Cola
Above: Print ads, radio spots, and TV commercials were only some of the ways Coca-Cola and other drinks gained fame. While much of pop's future was planned from the beginning, its destiny was fixed by those unexpected incidents that often propel a product into the limelight. Chief among these happy accidents were the impromptu, unrehearsed testimonials of prominent figures. If you could catch a president, pop star, or baseball hero downing a drink and freeze the moment in a photo, your sales were sure to rally. When the Beatles landed in America and refreshed their thirst, they were fair game for the paparazzi. *Courtesy of The Coca-Cola Company*

Ike Likes Coke
Above: While the political slogan for the thirty-fourth President of the United States, Dwight D. Eisenhower, was "I Like Ike," his personal slogan might very well have been "Ike Likes Coke!" During Ike's term, the world saw the end of the Korean War, the Supreme Court rule against racial segregation, the launch of the first space satellite, the inauguration of jet passenger service, the first atomic power plant, and the completion of the St. Lawrence Seaway. During it all, the formula for Coca-Cola remained the same and public demand never waned. *Courtesy of The Coca-Cola Company*

A New Dog for 1964

Top: Decked out in a red coat trimmed with white fur, black belt with buckle, and boots, the Santa Claus of artist Haddon Sundblom's imagination hits full stride in this 1964 Coca-Cola ad. Like a reincarnated superhero, old Santa had become a new creation, evolving light-years from the Saint Nicholas concept that prevailed in early America. *Coolstock.com Advertising Archives*

Santa and His Elves, 1960

Bottom: In 1960, the Santa and his elves ad received major magazine coverage. This happy scene was printed in *Look, Time, the Saturday Evening Post, Sports Illustrated, National Geographic,* and *Life* magazine. Where did the concept of Santa come from? Colonists from Holland imported the traditions of Saint Nicholas to America. Nicholas was the bishop of Myra who exhibited a great deal of generosity—especially when it came to children. He was elevated to the position of patron saint of children, and subsequently, people in many European countries reserved a day to remember him (and to pass out gifts to those in need). Unfortunately, people in the States were unable to pronounce the moniker correctly, and it was eventually corrupted to "Santa Claus." *Coolstock.com Advertising Archives*

Coca-Cola Drive-In Soda Couple

Above, left: Back during the days of carhops and curbside service, the Coca-Cola brand was synonymous with dining in your automobile. During the 1950s and 1960s, car couples spent many an evening parked at the local eatery, dining on hamburgers, chomping on French fries, slurping down milkshakes, and sipping on an ice-cold glass of Coke. In those days of tail fins and convertibles, Styrofoam and paper cups were unheard of—only the distinctive bell-shaped Coca-Cola glasses were suitable for serving. *Coolstock.com Collection*

Coca-Cola at the Salon

Above, right: By 1965, pop artists like Andy Warhol and Roy Lichtenstein were redefining the way America looked at art and advertising. The result was a transmogrification of both arenas, one affecting the other. Ad agencies of the time followed these trends, producing a number of interesting ads, including this high-tech, 1965 beauty salon image for Coca-Cola. *Coolstock.com Advertising Archives*

It's the Real Thing Dragster

Right: Drag racing came into its own during the 1970s. No longer a fringe activity as it once was during the 50s, racing was now a real, respectable sport with major sponsors (note the equipment manufacturers and Coca-Cola logo on the side of the dragster). Like Coke, drag racing was "The real thing." *Coolstock.com Advertising Archives*

1980s Coke Calendars

Bottom: During the 1980s, it appeared as if Coca-Cola was returning to tried and true advertising themes it had used in the past. Family and friends, and real relationships with other people worked quite nicely with the new "Coke is it" slogan. Coke was now an integral part of American culture, the "it" that binds family gatherings, favorite holidays, co-workers, and childhood fun together. *Courtesy of The Coca-Cola Company*

Coca-Cola Bottles on Wall

Facing page, top: Since its inception, the shapely Coca-Cola bottle has been a powerful symbol of sales for the company. Discernible even in the dark, the curvaceous contour has been used on signs and billboards—in both an idealized—and realistic form. It's no wonder that modern artists worldwide have taken the image and turned it on its ear, forcing the rest of us to look upon it in new and different ways. ©2001 Mike Witzel, Coolstock.com

It's the real thing. Coke.

Before a great run, the real thing. An ice-cold Coca-Cola. That's the way it should be.

Coke is it!

Like The Time That You Spend With Your Family And Friends

Max Headroom Coke Lunchbox

Below: To compete with Pepsi's "Choice of a New Generation" and "Pepsi Challenge" ad campaigns of the late 1980s, Coke employed the computer-generated personality Max Headroom. The hip pitchman became a visible advocate for the New Coke formula as a television program featuring his quirky visage gained its own loyal audience (aired during 1986–1987). Critics lauded the New Coke commercials as one of the most original ad campaigns of 1987, despite the failure of the New Coke formula. Max coined the famous tag lines "Don't say the P-word" and the still-used "Catch the wave." A lunchbox bearing his likeness and the Coca-Cola brand was just one of many promotional items produced during the campaign. *Photo Courtesy of the Author's Collection*

Cool Polar Bear Ad

Right: During the "Always Coca-Cola" advertising campaign of the 1990s, television commercials for Coca-Cola depicted computer-generated polar bears enjoying the beverage. Although the animated images were striking, the concept behind them was by no means new. A commercial artist had already experimented with the bear and bottle image in 1920s Paris. In that version, the polar bears standing on hind legs fed the sun a cold bottle of the drink. *Courtesy of The Coca-Cola Company*

Harley-Davidson Promotion

Bottom: "Time to Refuel . . . With Real Cola Taste" was the slogan utilized for a cross-country Coca-Cola promotional tour in 1996. As part of the tour, a caravan of two support vehicles carried promotional drink coolers and three Harley-Davidson motorcycles (equipped with specially built Coca-Cola bottle sidecars) across the country. At select supermarket locations, both the bikes and the drinks were unloaded and put on display. Patrons received free bottles of Coca-Cola and a chance to drool over the outrageous two-wheelers. *©2001 Mike Witzel, Coolstock.com*

Suggested Reading

Allen, Frederick. *Secret Formula*. New York: Harper Collins Publishers, Inc., 1994.

Armstrong, David and Elizabeth Metzger Armstrong. *The Great American Medicine Show*. New York: Prentice Hall, 1991.

Brown, John Hull. *Early American Beverages*. Rutland, Vermont: Charles. E. Tuttle Company, 1966.

Calhoun, Mary. *Medicine Show: Conning People and Making Them Like It*. New York: Harper & Row Publishers, 1976.

Carson, Gerald. *One for a Man, Two for a Horse*. New York: Bramhall House, n.d.

Cash, G. Howard. All In Flavour: *The Canadian Soft Drink Industry and Its Association* 1942–1992. Toronto: The Canadian Soft Drink Association, 1992.

Dickson, Paul. *The Great American Ice Cream Book*. New York: Galahad Books, 1972.

Dietz, Lawrence. *Soda Pop: The History, Advertising, Art and Memorabilia of Soft Drinks in America*. New York: Simon and Schuster, 1973.

Ebert, Albert Ethelbert, Ph.D. and A. Emil Hiss, Ph.G. *The Standard Formulary: A Collection of Over Four Thousand Formulas*. Chicago, Illinois: G. P. Englehard & Co., 1896.

Enrico, Roger and Jesse Kornbluth. *The Other Guy Blinked: How Pepsi Won the Cola Wars*. New York: Bantam Books, 1986.

Erlbach, Arlene. *Soda Pop: How It's Made*. Minneapolis, Minnesota: Lerner Publications Company, 1994.

Ferguson, Frank L. *Efficient Drug Store Management*. New York: Fairchild Publications, Inc., 1969.

Foster, Steven and Yue Chongxi. *Herbal Emissaries*. Rochester, Vermont: Healing Arts Press, 1992.

Funderburg, Ann Cooper. *Chocolate, Strawberry, and Vanilla: A History of American Ice Cream*. Bowling Green, Ohio: Bowling Green State University Press, 1995.

Furnell, Dennis. *Health from the Hedgerow*. London, England: B. T. Batsford Ltd., 1985.

Gazan, M. H. *Flavours and Essences*. London, England: Chapman & Hall Ltd., 1936.

Grimes, William. *Straight Up or On the Rocks: A Cultural History of American Drink*. New York: Simon & Schuster, 1993.

Hechtlinger, Adelaide. *The Great Patent Medicine Era, or Without Benefit of Doctor*. New York: Grosset & Dunlap, Inc., 1970.

Hoy, Anne. *The First Hundred Years:* Coca-Cola. Atlanta, Georgia: The Coca-Cola Company, 1986.

Jacobs, Morris B., Ph.D. *Synthethic Food Adjuncts*. New York: D. Van Nostrand Company, Inc., 1947.

Kremers, Edward. *Kremers' and Urdang's History of Pharmacy*. Philadelphia, Pennsylvania: Lippincott, 1976.

Lloyd, Everette and Mary Lloyd. *Pepsi-Cola Collectibles, With Price Guide*. Atglen, Pennsylvania: Schiffer Publishing Ltd., 1993.

Lofland, Cheryl Harris. *The National Soft Drink Association: A Tradition of Service*. Washington, D.C.: National Soft Drink Association, 1986.

Mack, Walter with Peter Buckley. *No Time Lost*. New York: Atheneum, 1982.

Marsh, Thomas. *The Official Guide to Collecting Applied Color Label Soda Bottles*. Youngstown, Ohio: Thomas E. Marsh, Inc., 1992.

Martin, Milward W. *Twelve Full Ounces*. New York: Holt, Rinehart and Winston, 1969.

Mayo, P. Randolph, Jr. *Coca-Cola Heritage*. Austin, Texas: Best Printing Company, Inc., 1990.

McCutheon, Marc. *Everyday Life in the 1800s*. Cincinnati, Ohio: Writer's Digest Books, 1993.

Merory, Joseph. *Food Flavorings: Composition, Manufacture, and Use*. Westport, Connecticut: The AVI Publishing Company, Inc., 1960.

Morrison, Tom. Root Beer: *Advertising and Collectibles*. West Chester, Pennsylvania: Schiffer Publishing, 1992.

Mowrey, Daniel B., Ph.D. *The Scientific Validation of Herbal Medicine*. Cormorant Books, 1986.

Munsey, Cecil. *The Illustrated Guide to the Collectibles of Coca-Cola*. New York: Hawthorn Books, Inc., 1972.

Oliver, Thomas. *The Real Coke, The Real Story*. New York: Random House, 1986.

Palazzini, Fiora Steinbach. *Coca-Cola Superstar*. New York: Barron's Educational Series, 1989.

Paul, John R. and Paul W. Parmalee. *Soft Drink Bottling, A History with Special Reference to Illinois*. Springfield, Illinois: Illinois State Museum Society, 1973.

Pepsi-Cola Company. "History and Milestones." PepsiCo Inc., 1995.

Pepsi-Cola Company. "Pepsi-Cola Advertising Timeline." PepsiCo Inc., 1995.

Petretti, *Alan. Petretti's Coca-Cola Collectibles Price Guide, The Encyclopedia of Coca-Cola Collectibles*. Radnor, Pennsylvania: Wallace Homestead, 1992.

Pomeroy, Ralph. *The Ice Cream Connection*. New York: Paddington Press Ltd., Two Continents Publishing Group, 1975.

Potter, Frank N. *The Book of Moxie*. Paducah, Kentucky: Collector Books, 1987.

Potter, Frank N. *The Moxie Mystique*. Paducah, Kentucky: Moxiebooks, 1981.

Poundstone, William. *Big Secrets*. New York: William Morrow and Company, Inc., 1983.

Rawcliffe, Carole. *Medicine & Society in Later Medieval England*. United Kingdom: Alan Sutton Publishing Limited, 1995.

Riley, John J. *A History of the American Soft Drink Industry*. Washington, D.C.: American Bottlers of Carbonated Beverages, 1958.

Sachorow, Stanley. *Symbols of Trade*. New York: Art Direction Book Company, 1982.

Shih, Ko Ching, Ph.D., and C. Ying Shih, Ph.D. *American Soft Drink Industry and the Carbonated Beverage Market*. Brookfield, Wisconsin: W. A. Krueger Co., 1965.

Shimko, Phyllis. *Sarsaparilla Bottle Encyclopedia*. Oregon: Andrew & Phyllis Shimko, 1969.

Simmons, Douglas A. *Schweppes: The First 200 Years*. Washington, D.C.: Acropolis Books, 1983.

Swanner, Grace Maguire, M.D. *Saratoga Queen of Spas*. Utica, New York: North Country Books, Inc., 1988.

Tchudi, Stephen N. *Soda Poppery: The History of Soft Drinks in America*. New York: Charles Scribner's Sons, 1986.

Time-Life Books, by the Editors. *This Fabulous Century: Prelude 1870– 1900*. New York: Time-Life Books, 1970.

Tufts, James W. *The Manufacturing and Bottling of Carbonated Beverages*. Fort Davis, Texas: Frontier Book Company, 1969.

Vehling, Bill and Michael Hunt. *Pepsi-Cola Collectibles*. Gas City, Indiana: L-W Book Sales, 1986.

Walker, Mildred. "Crown Cork & Seal Co., Inc." Unpublished, undated manuscript.

Walker, Mildred. "Soft Drinks and Their Owners/Franchisers." Unpublished, undated manuscript.

Walter, Erich. *Manual for the Essence Industry*. New York: John Wiley & Sons, Inc., 1916.

Walters, Jeff. *Classic Soda Machines, A Field Reference and Price Guide*. Pollock Pines, California: Memory Lane, 1992.

Watkins. T. H. *The Great Depression*. New York: Little, Brown and Company, 1993.

Watters, Pat. *Coca-Cola: An Illustrated History*. Garden City, New York: Doubleday & Company, Inc., 1978.

Witzel, Michael Karl. *Drive-In Deluxe*. Osceola, Wisconsin: Motorbooks International, 1997.

Witzel, Michael Karl. *The American Drive-In: History and Folklore of the Drive-In Restaurant in American Car Culture*. Osceola, Wisconsin: Motorbooks International, 1994.

Wunderlich, Keith D. "Deliciously Different: The Vernor's Ginger Ale Story." Unpublished manuscript, 1996.

Young, James Harvey. *The Toadstool Millionaires: A Social History of Patent Medicines in America Before Federal Regulation*. Princeton, New Jersey: Princeton University Press, 1961.

Index

About the Authors

Michael Karl Witzel and Gyvel Young-Witzel are the authors of numerous books on American pop culture, including *Gas Stations Across America, The American Motel, The American Diner, Cruisin': Car Culture in America, The American Drive-In, The American Gas Station,* and *Soda Pop: From Miracle Medicine to Pop Culture.*

1957 Under the Umbrella
Left: The romance of youth comprised the theme for this 1957 calendar, one of many issued during the year. Times were good for Coca-Cola, and the printing of multiple calendars was part of the overall marketing blitz intended to gain a world-wide audience. *Courtesy of The Coca-Cola Company*

1957 Boating Girl
Right: Continuing in the outdoor activities theme that was promoted during 1957, Coca-Cola issued this boating-themed calendar as part of a series. Women were no longer depicted in social settings draped in evening gowns and furs, but in outdoor venues donning sporty garb. "Best-loved sparkling drink in all the world" and "Coke is just right" were two of the other ad slogans that made their debut when this calendar hung on the wall. *Courtesy of The Coca-Cola Company*